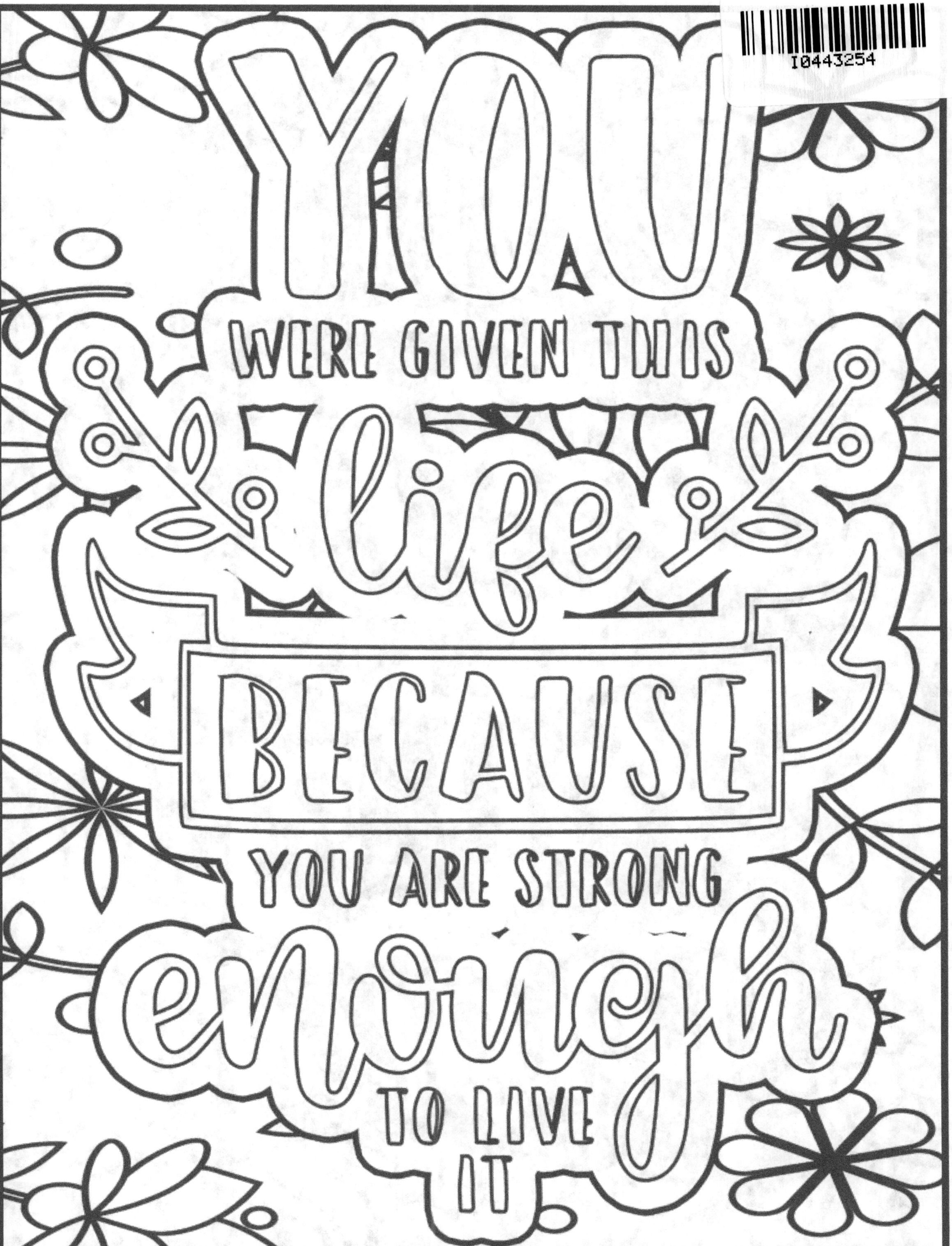
YOU
WERE GIVEN THIS
life
BECAUSE
YOU ARE STRONG
enough
TO LIVE
IT

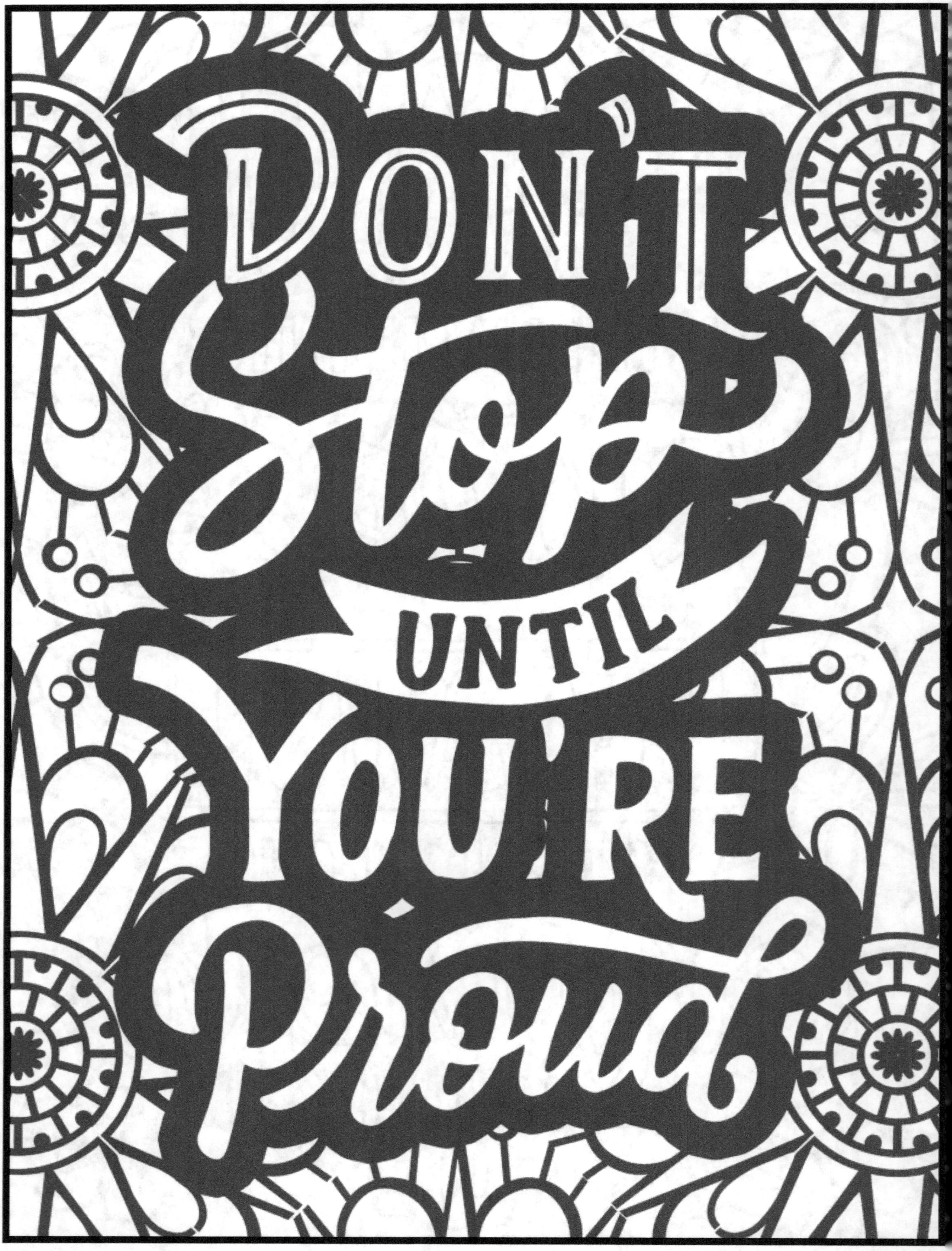
Don't
Stop
until
You're
Proud

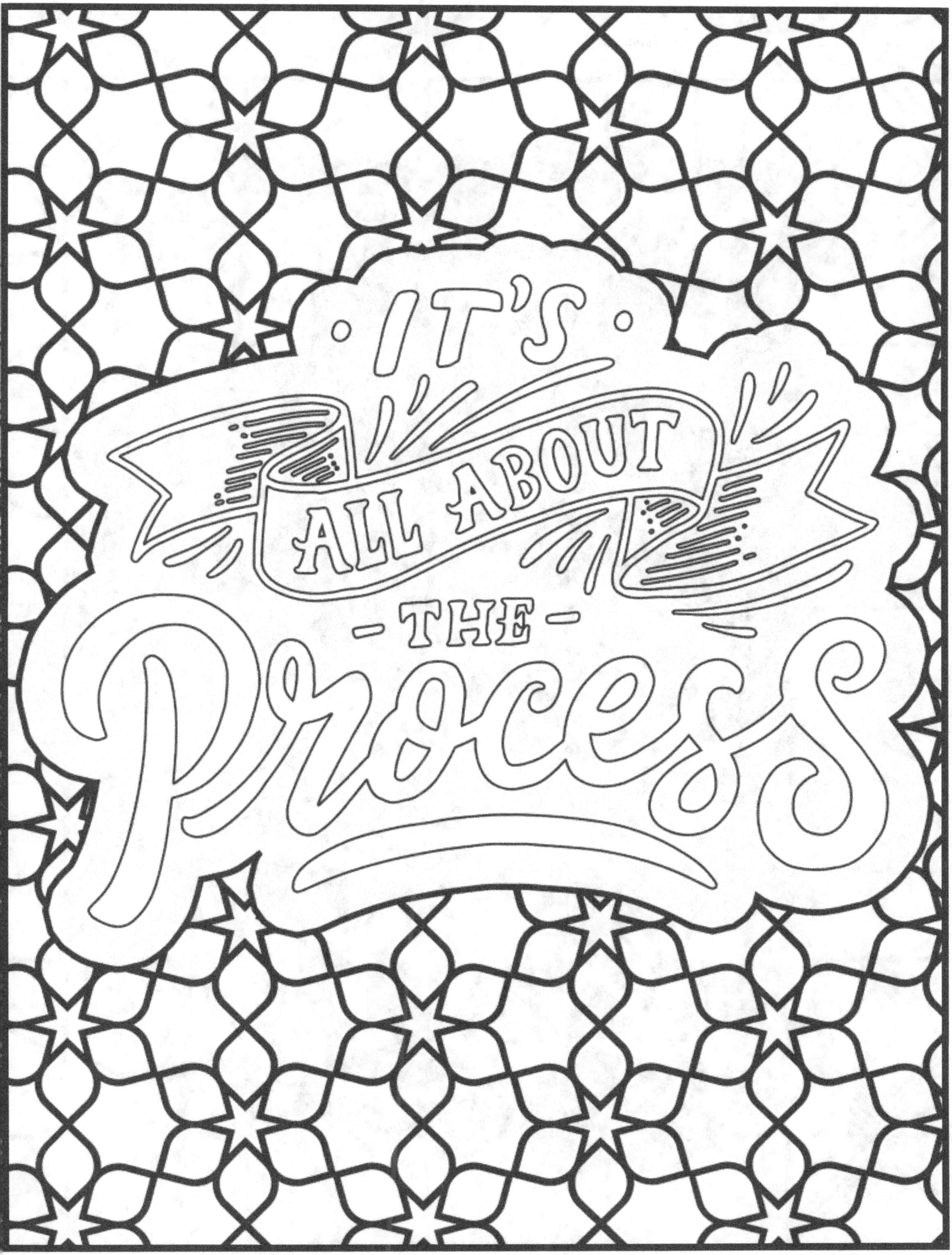
IT'S
ALL ABOUT
THE
Process

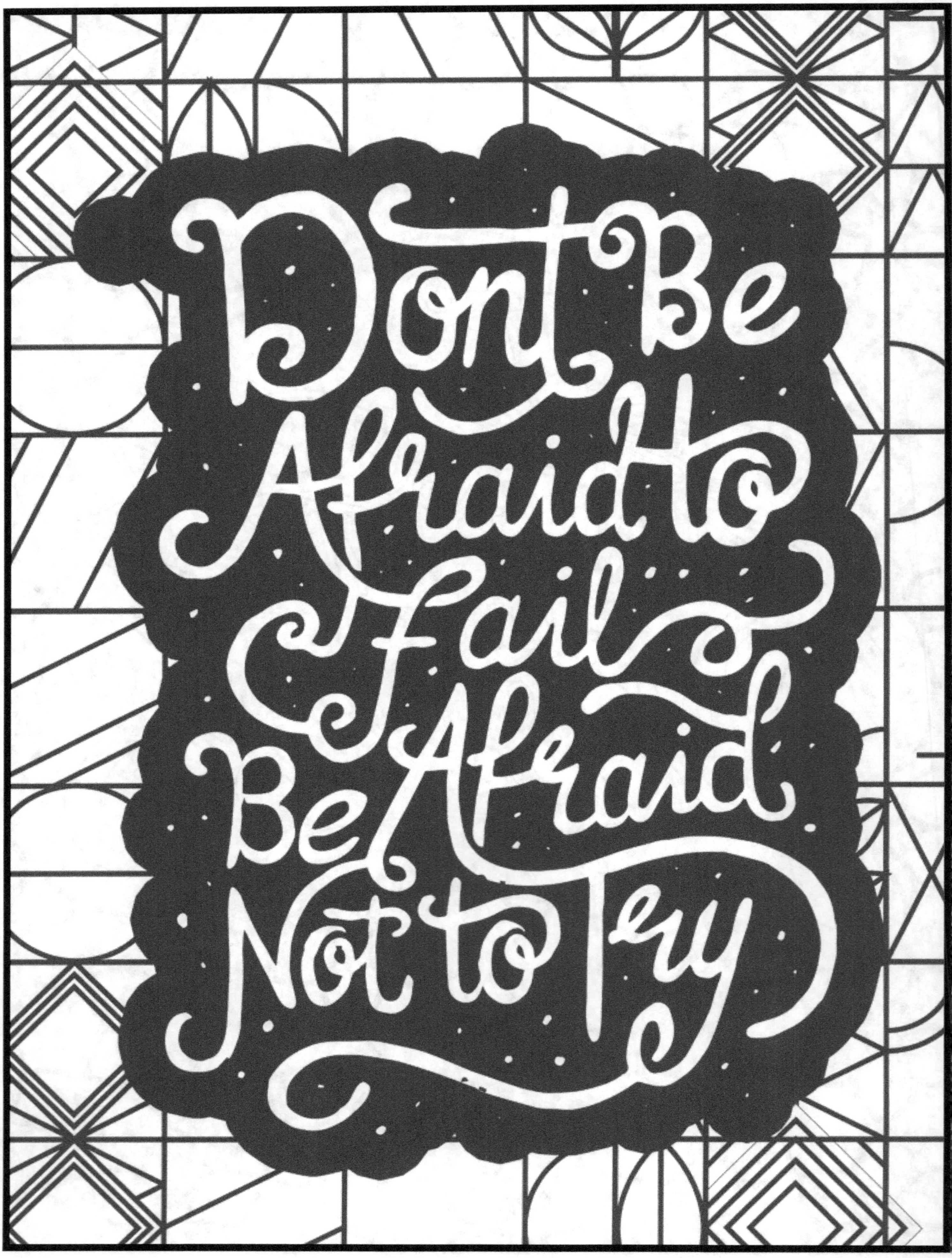
Dont Be
Afraid to
Fail
Be Afraid
Not to Try

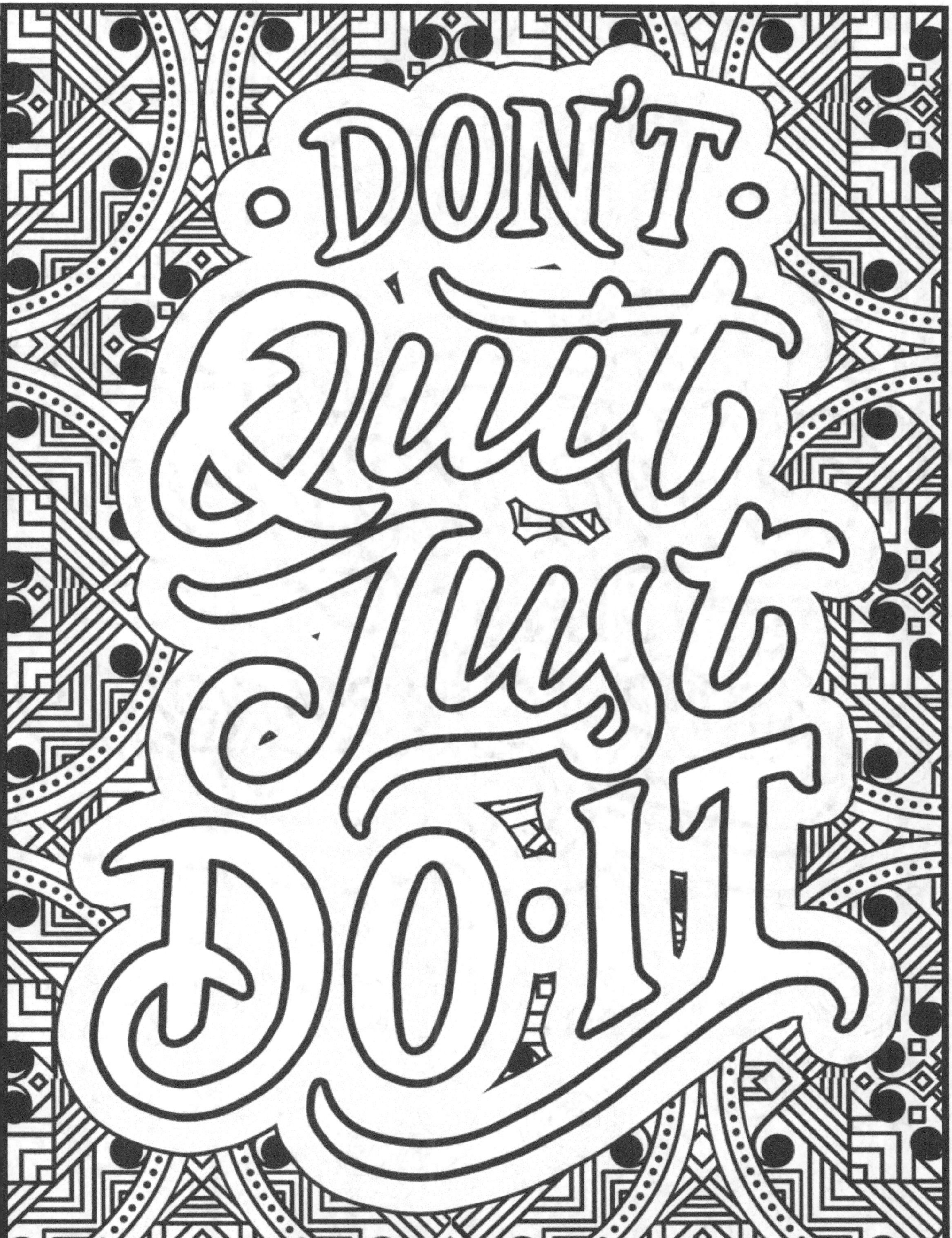
DON'T
Quit
Just
DO IT

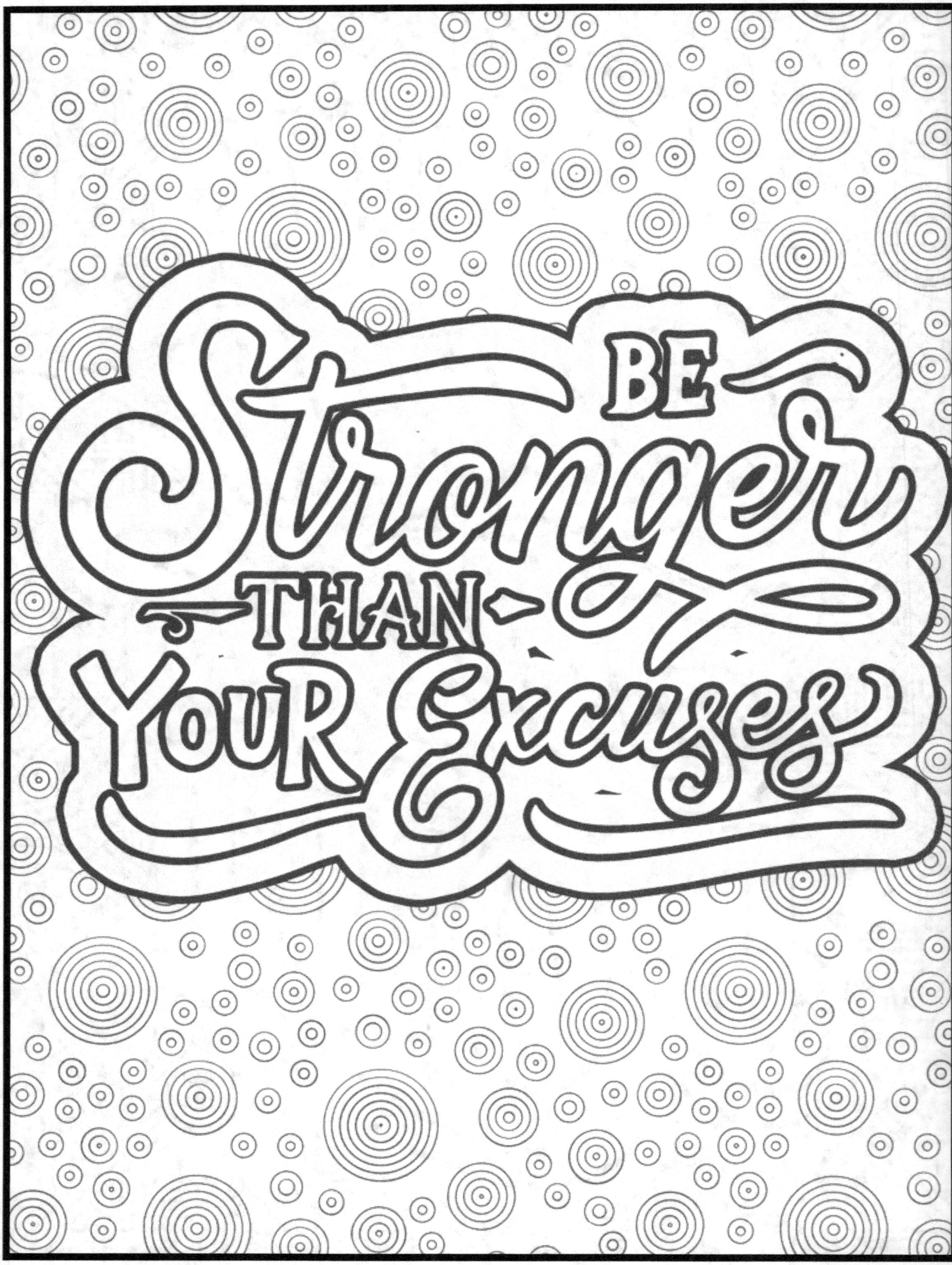

BE
Stronger
THAN
YOUR Excuses

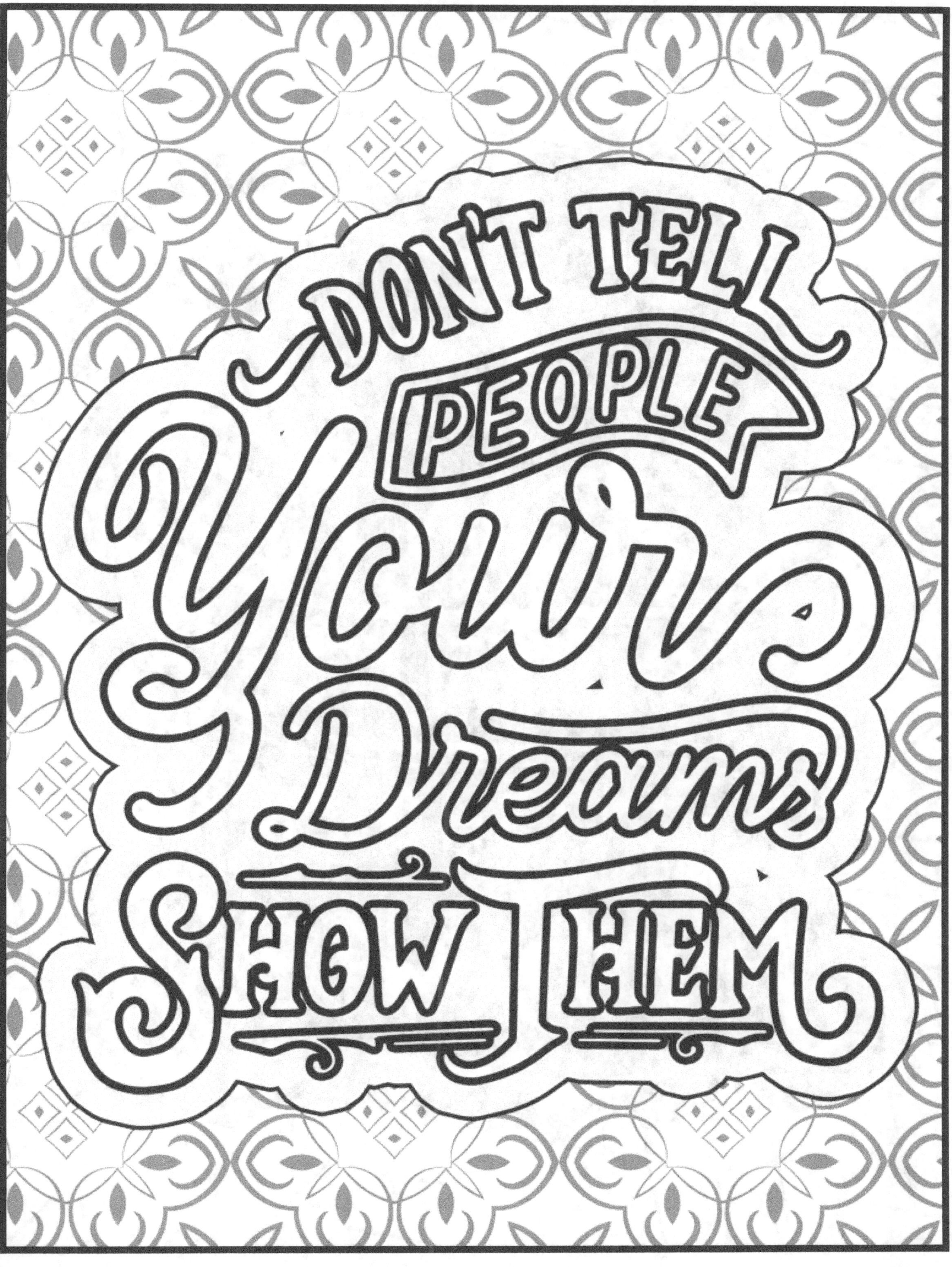
DON'T TELL
PEOPLE
Your
Dreams
SHOW THEM

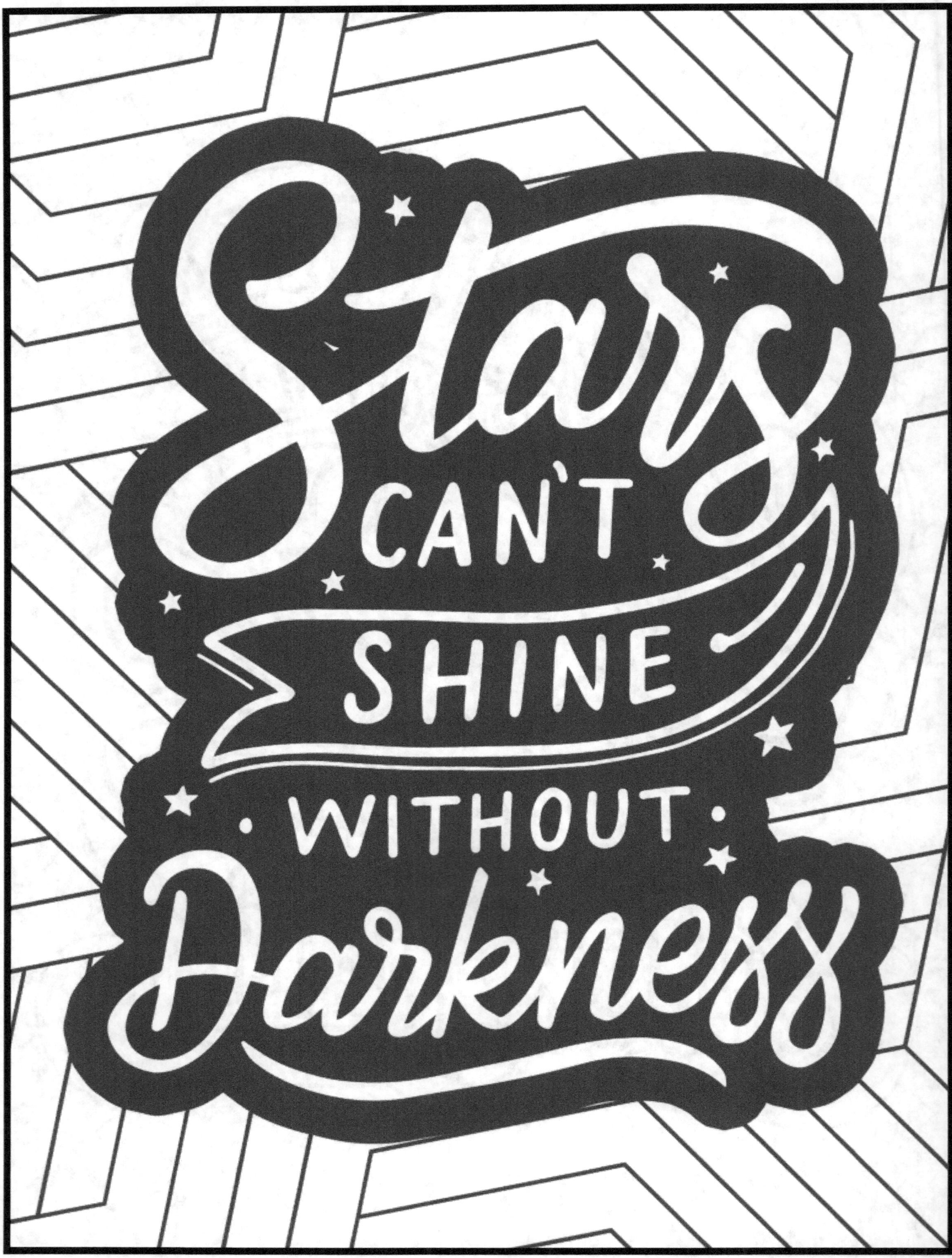
Stars
CAN'T
SHINE
WITHOUT
Darkness

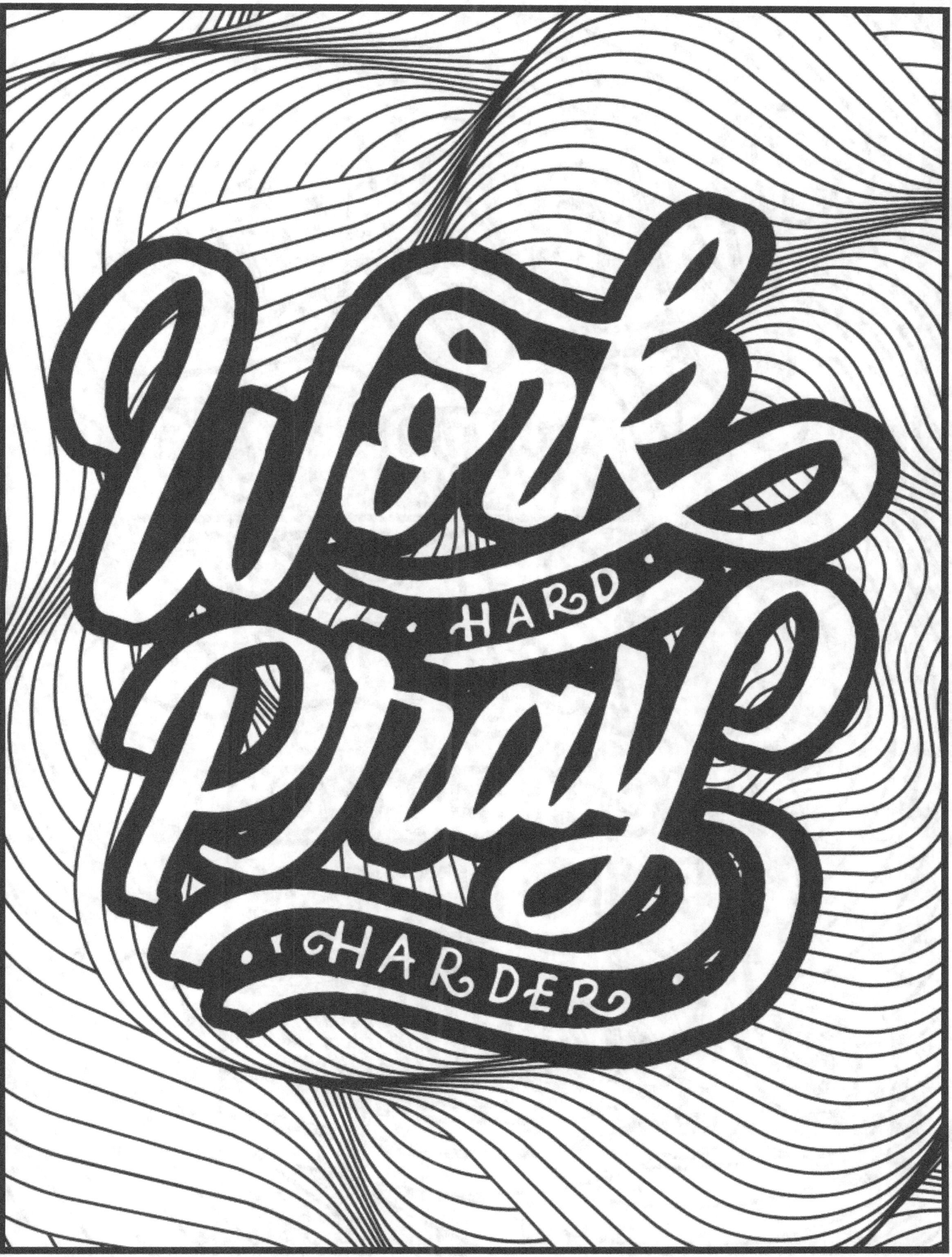
Work
HARD
Pray
HARDER

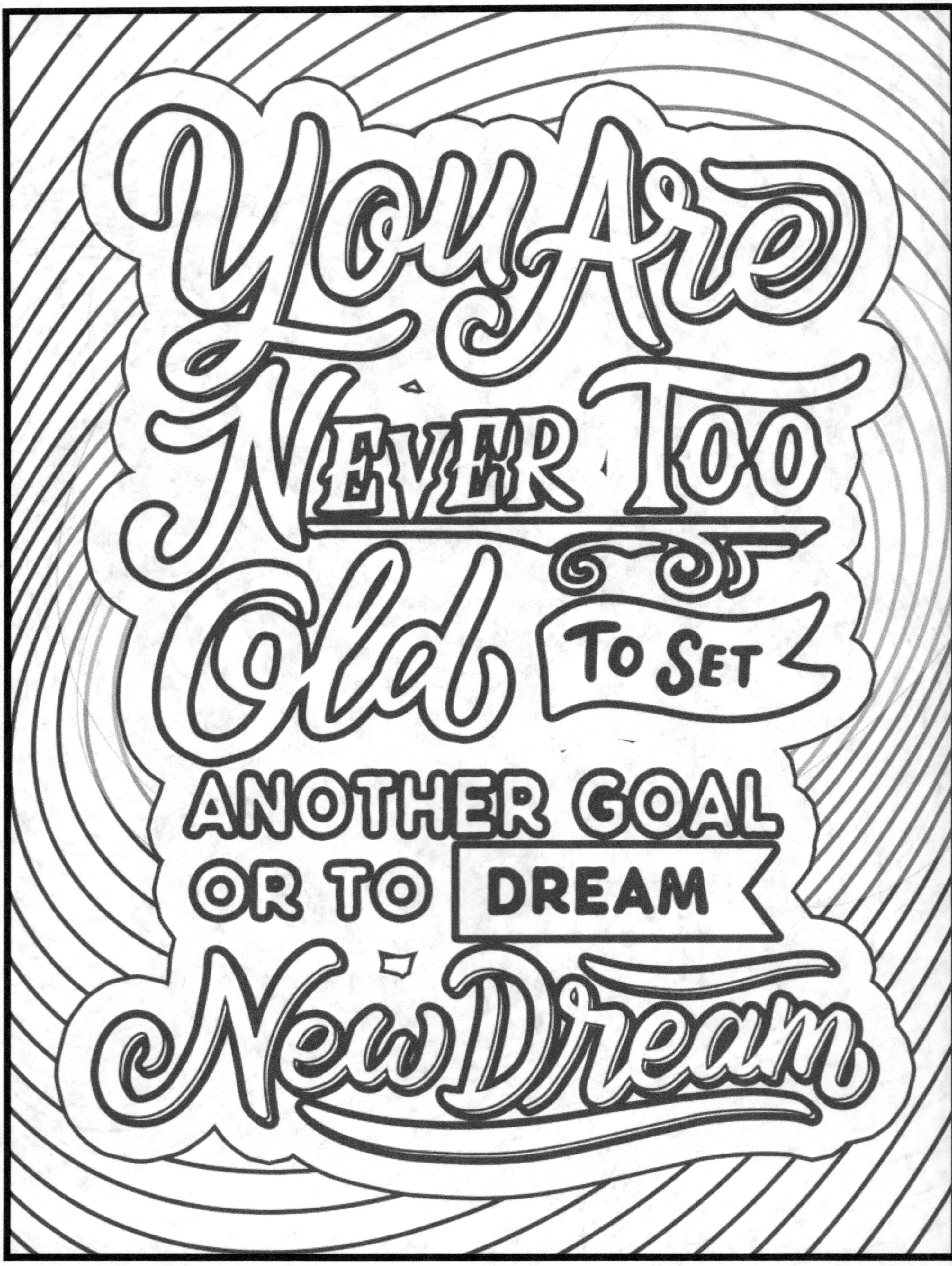
You Are
Never Too
Old To Set
ANOTHER GOAL
OR TO DREAM
A New Dream

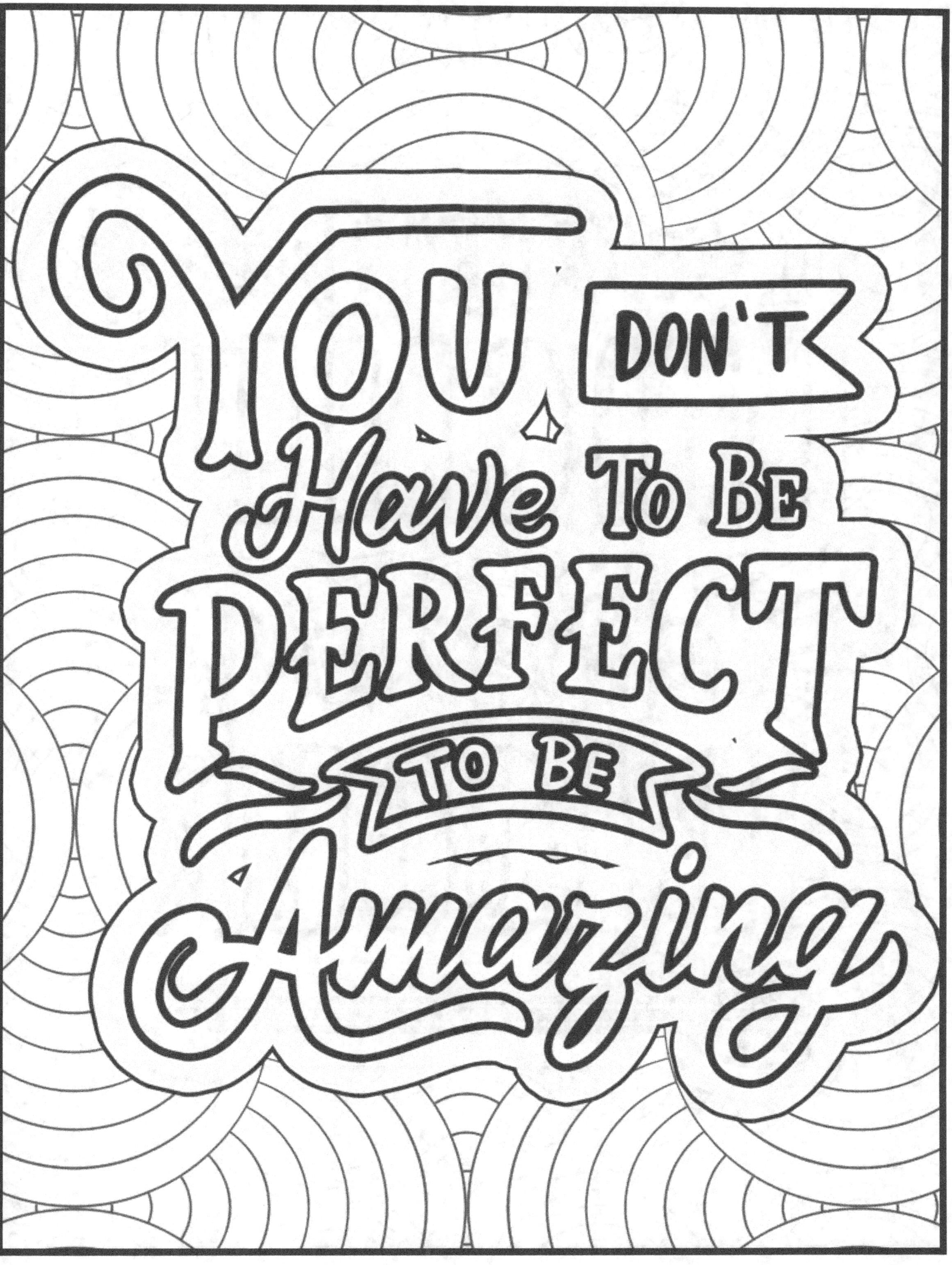
You don't
Have To Be
PERFECT
TO BE
Amazing

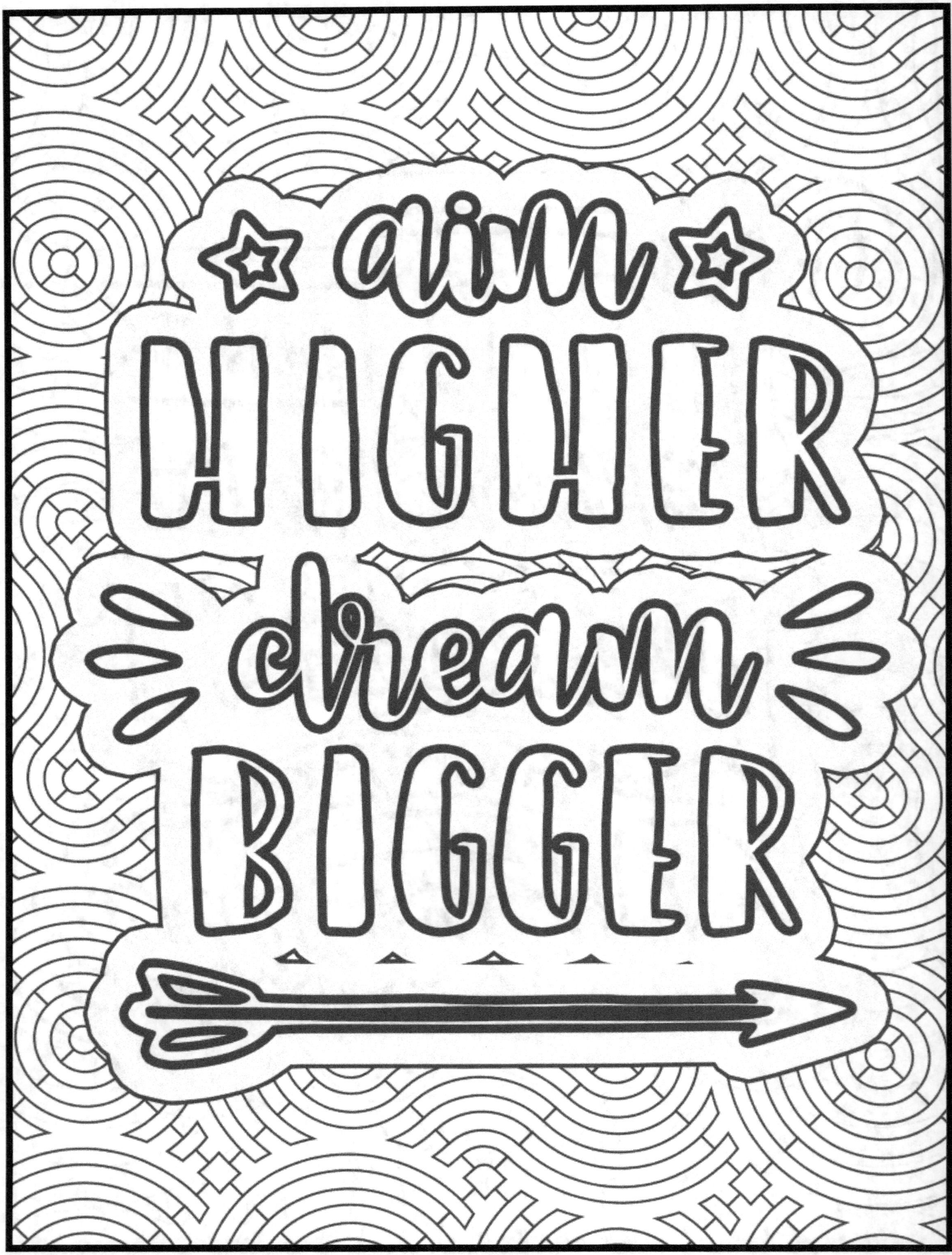
aim
HIGHER
dream
BIGGER

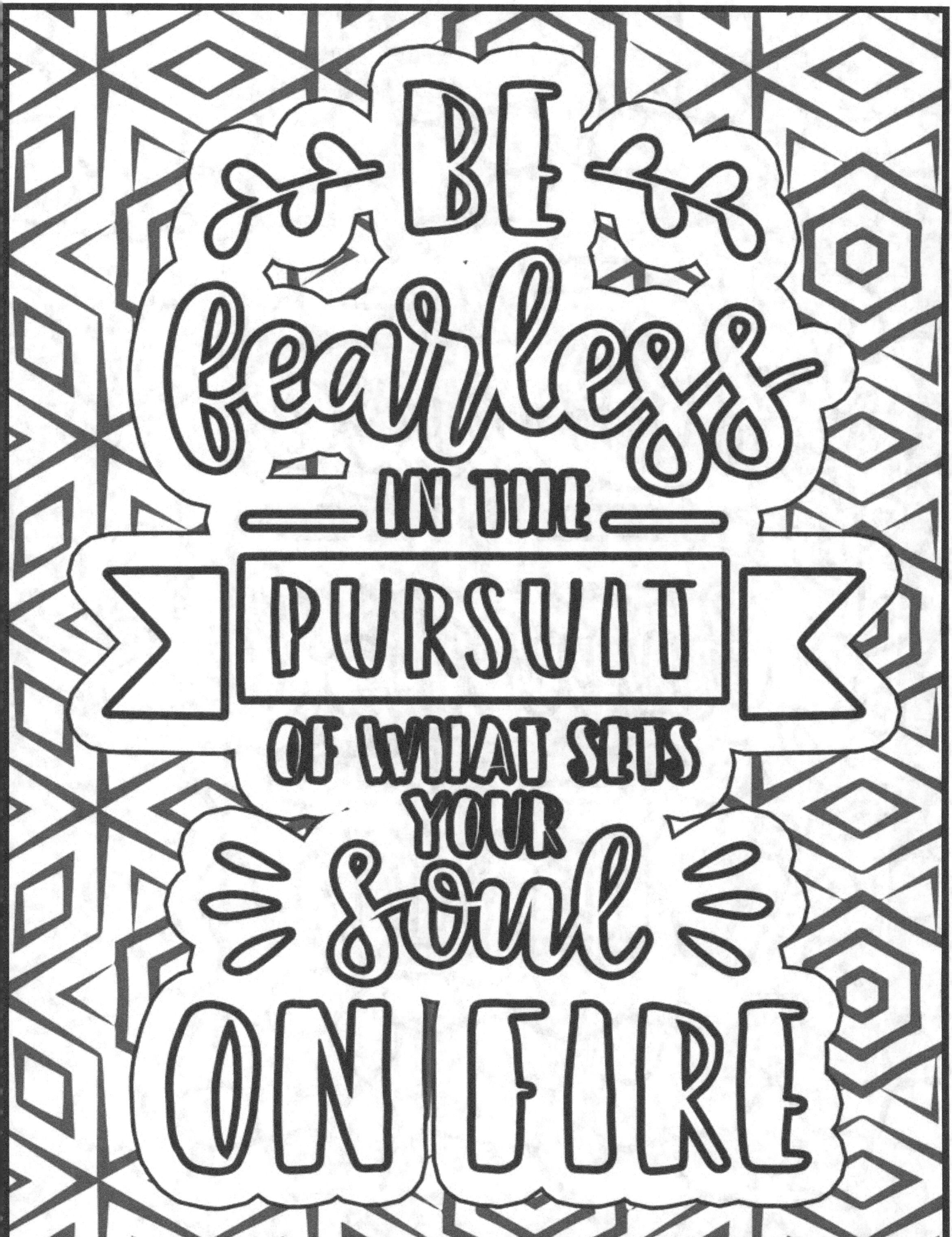
BE
fearless
IN THE
PURSUIT
OF WHAT SETS
YOUR
soul
ON FIRE

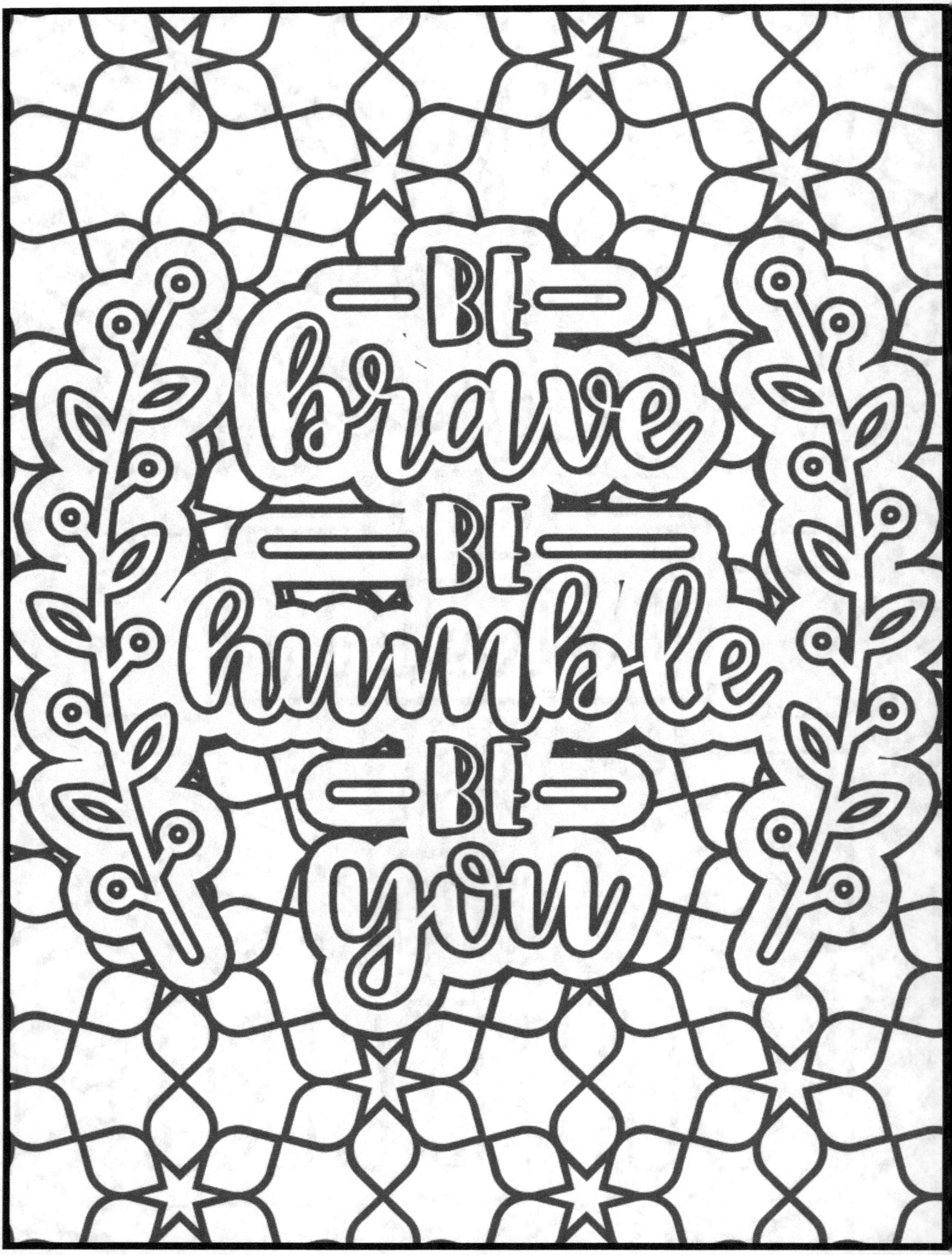
BE
brave
BE
humble
BE
you

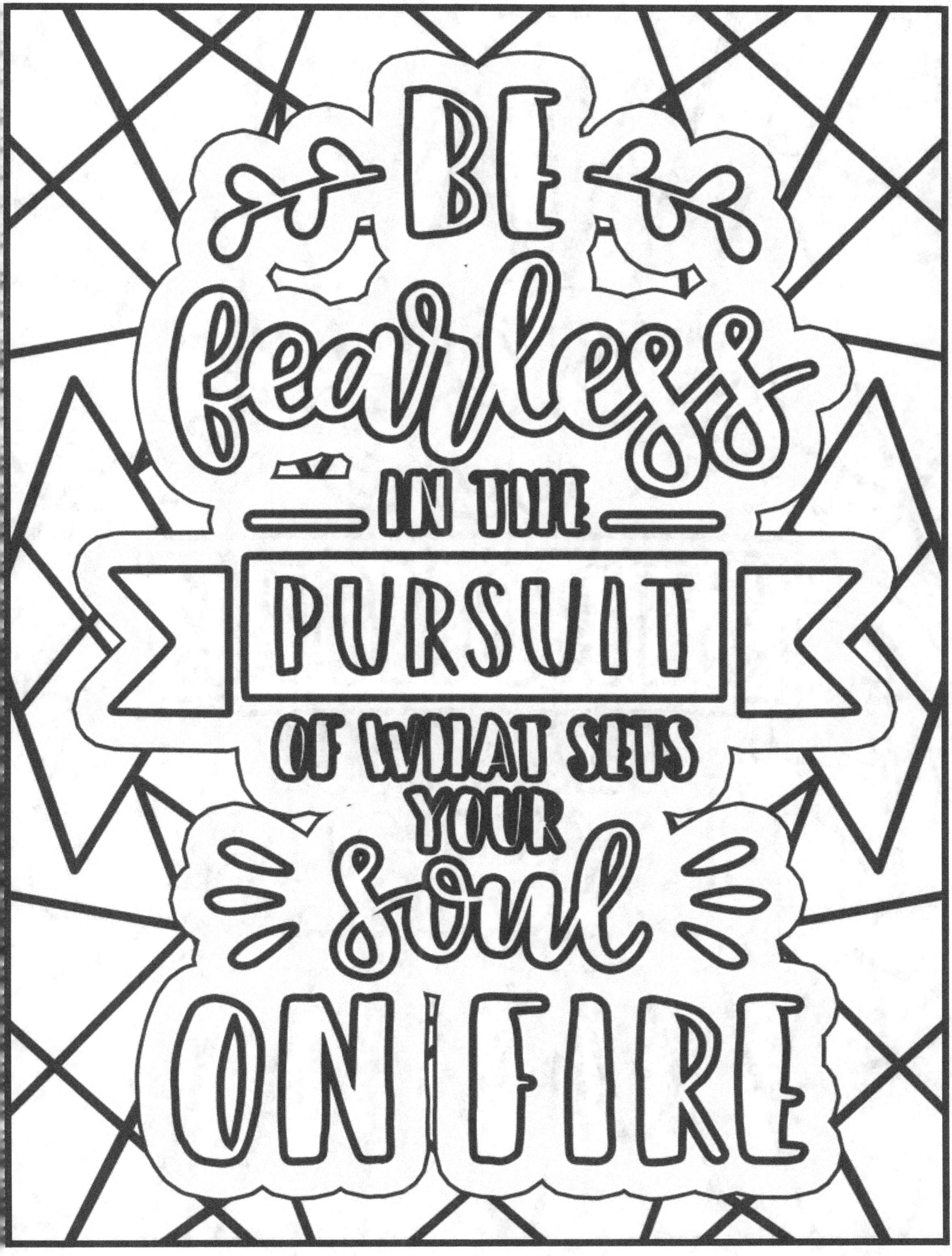
BE
fearless
IN THE
PURSUIT
OF WHAT SETS
YOUR
soul
ON FIRE

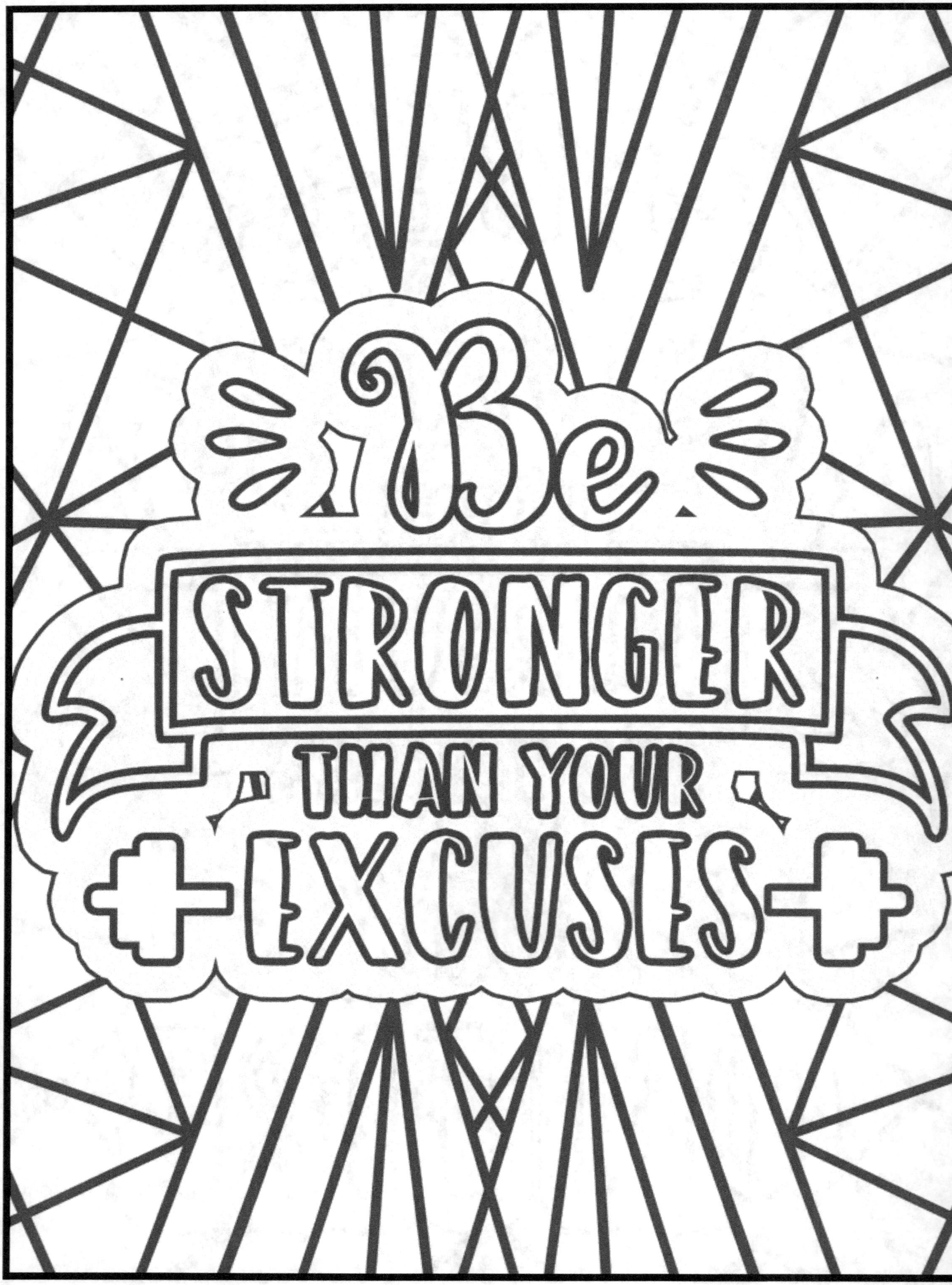
Be
STRONGER
THAN YOUR
EXCUSES

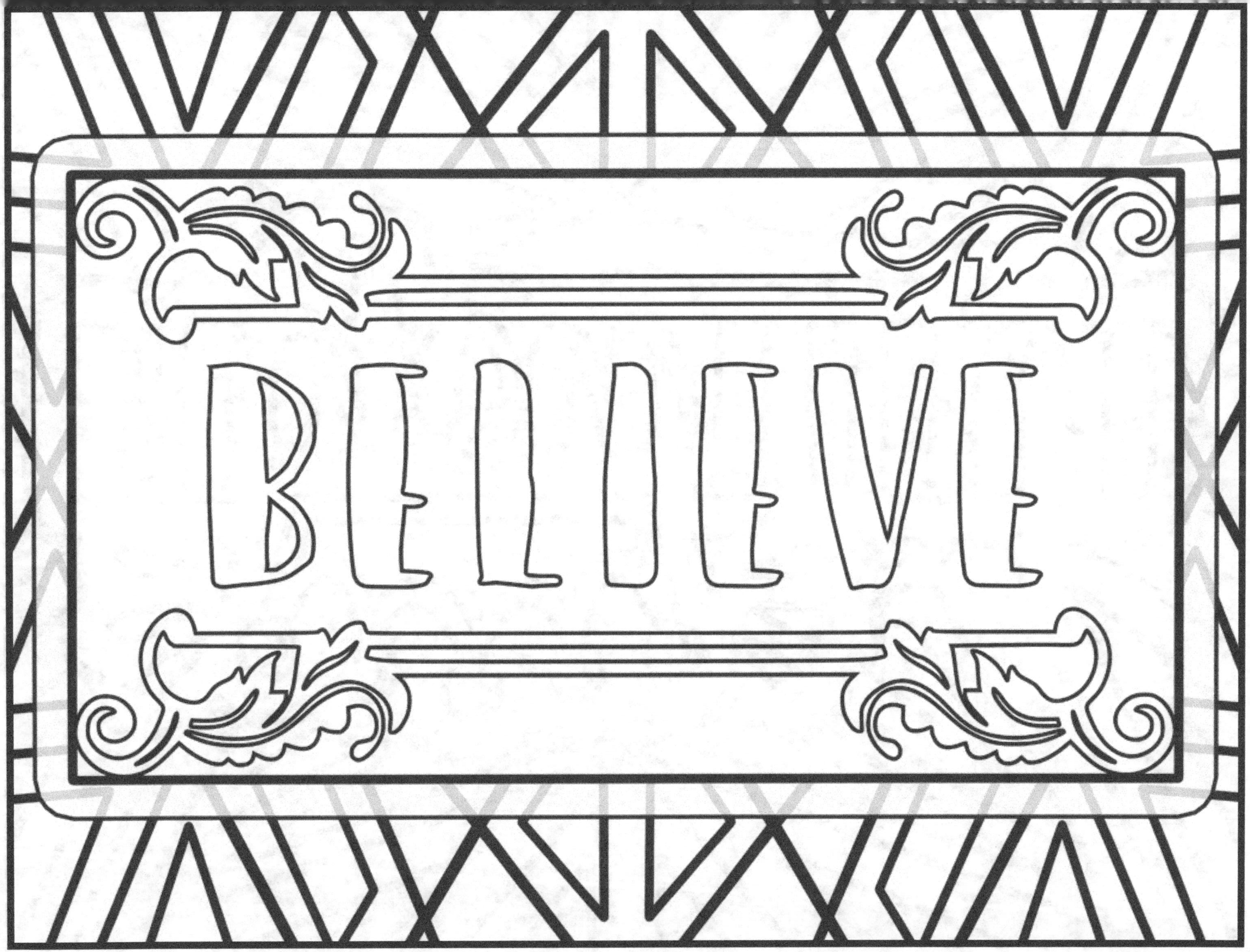
BELIEVE

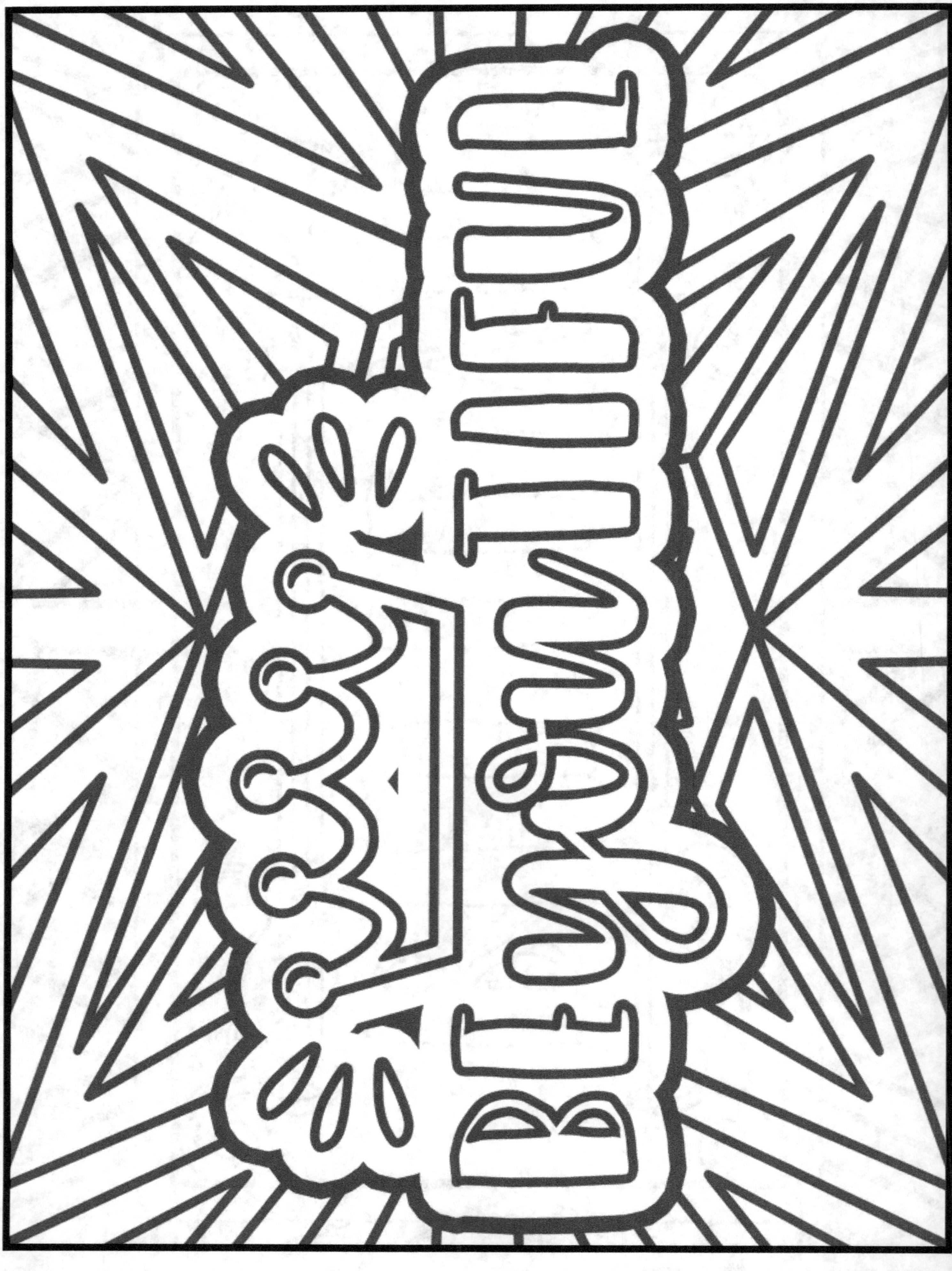
BEyouTIFUL

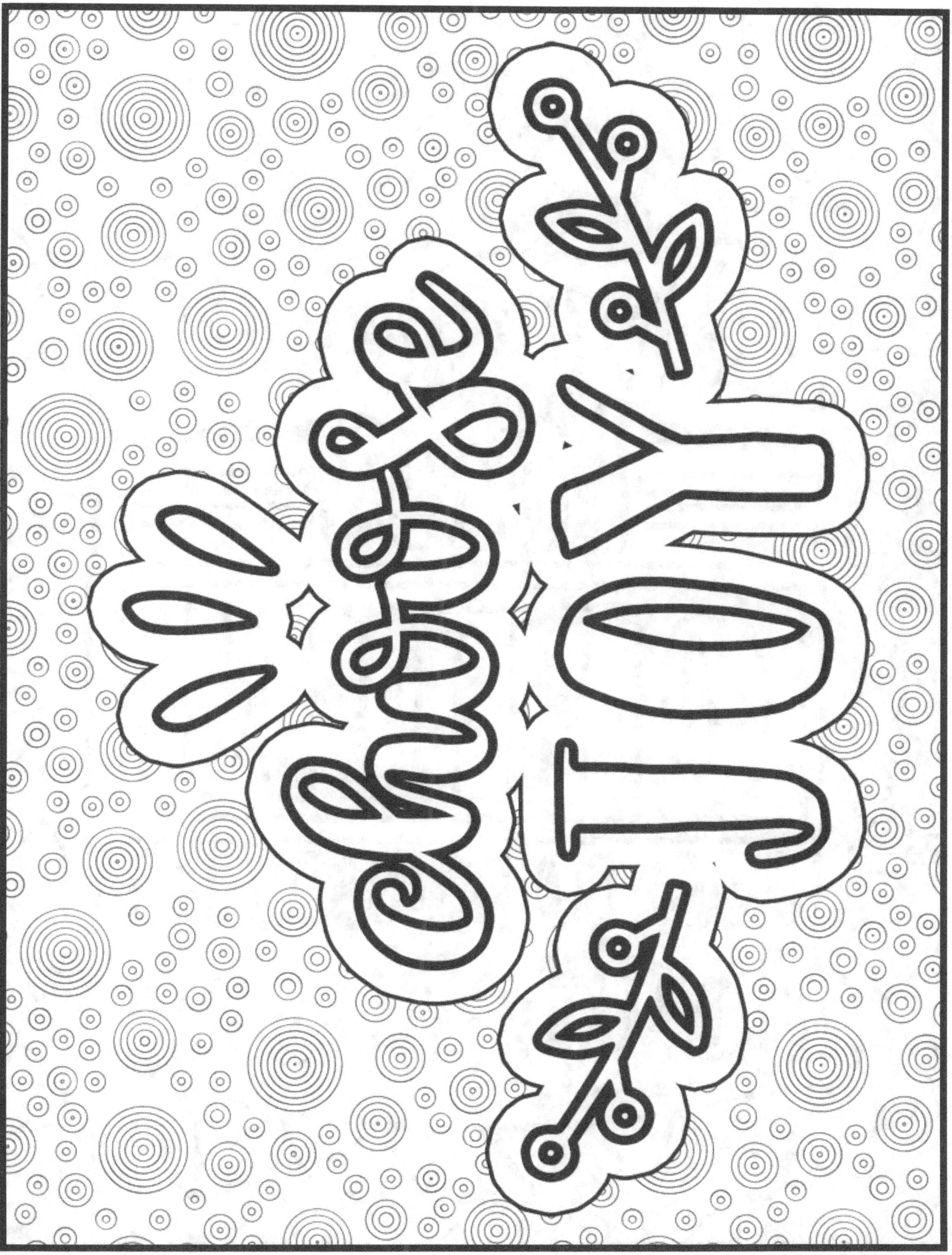
choose
JOY

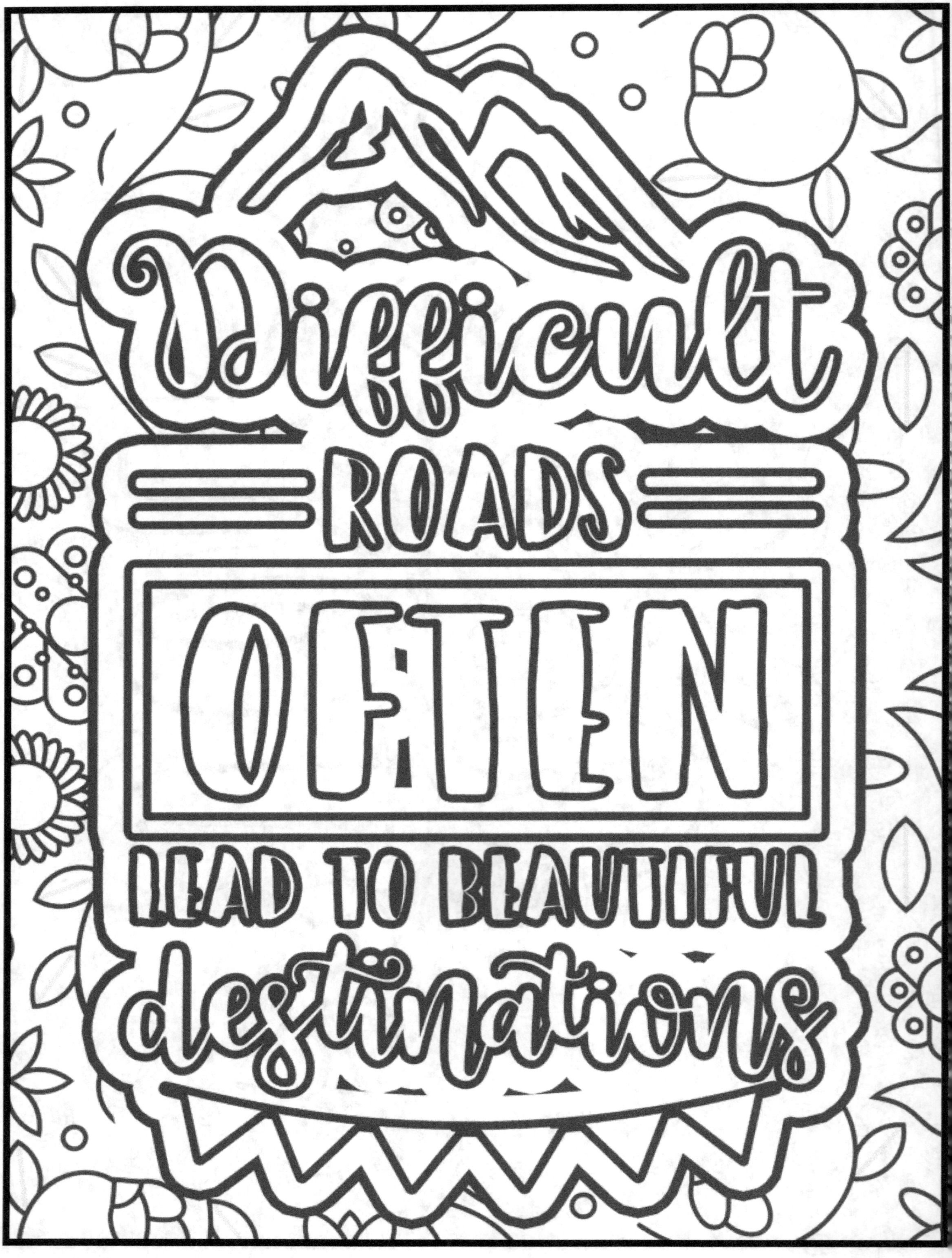
Difficult
ROADS
OFTEN
LEAD TO BEAUTIFUL
destinations

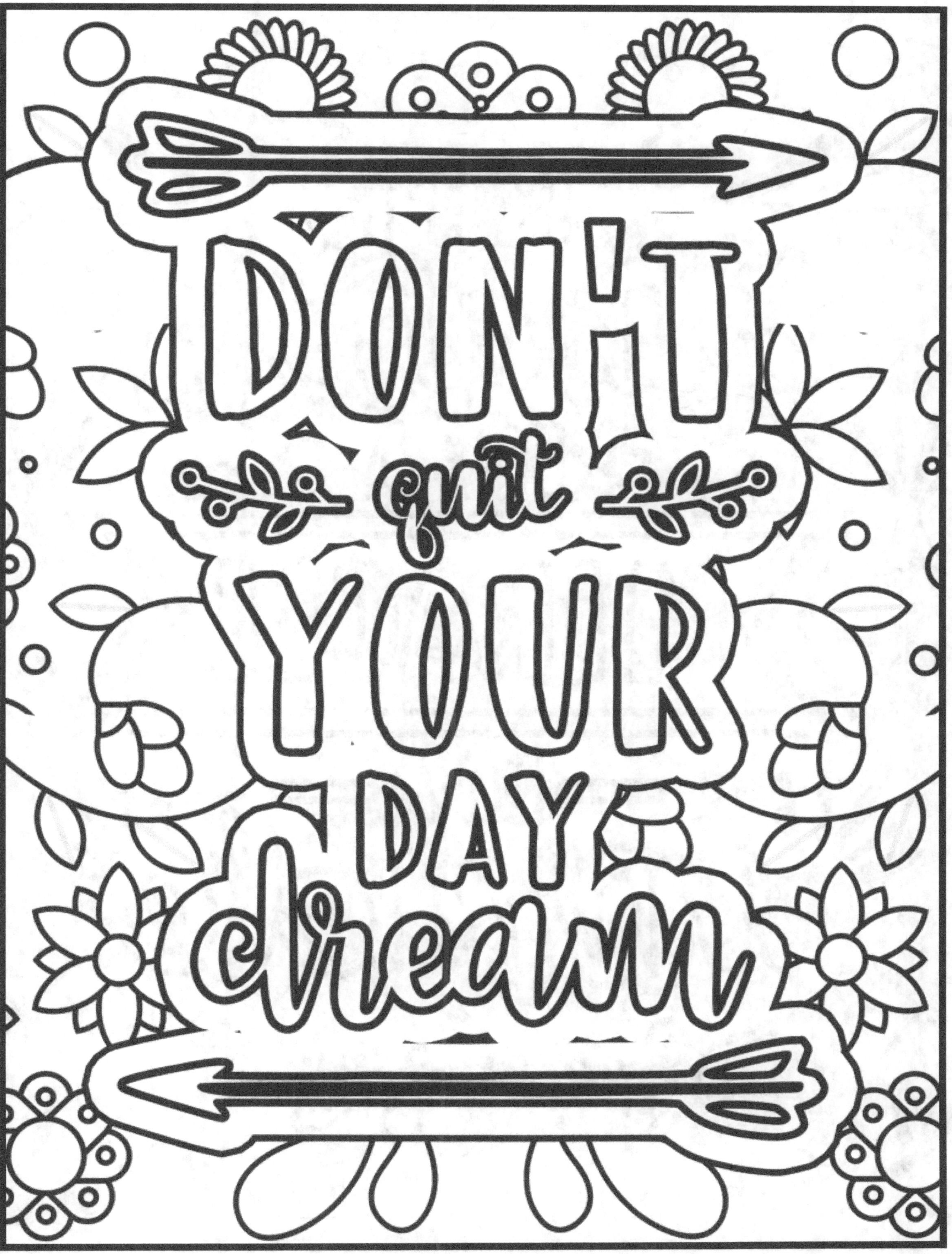
DON'T
quit
YOUR
DAY
dream

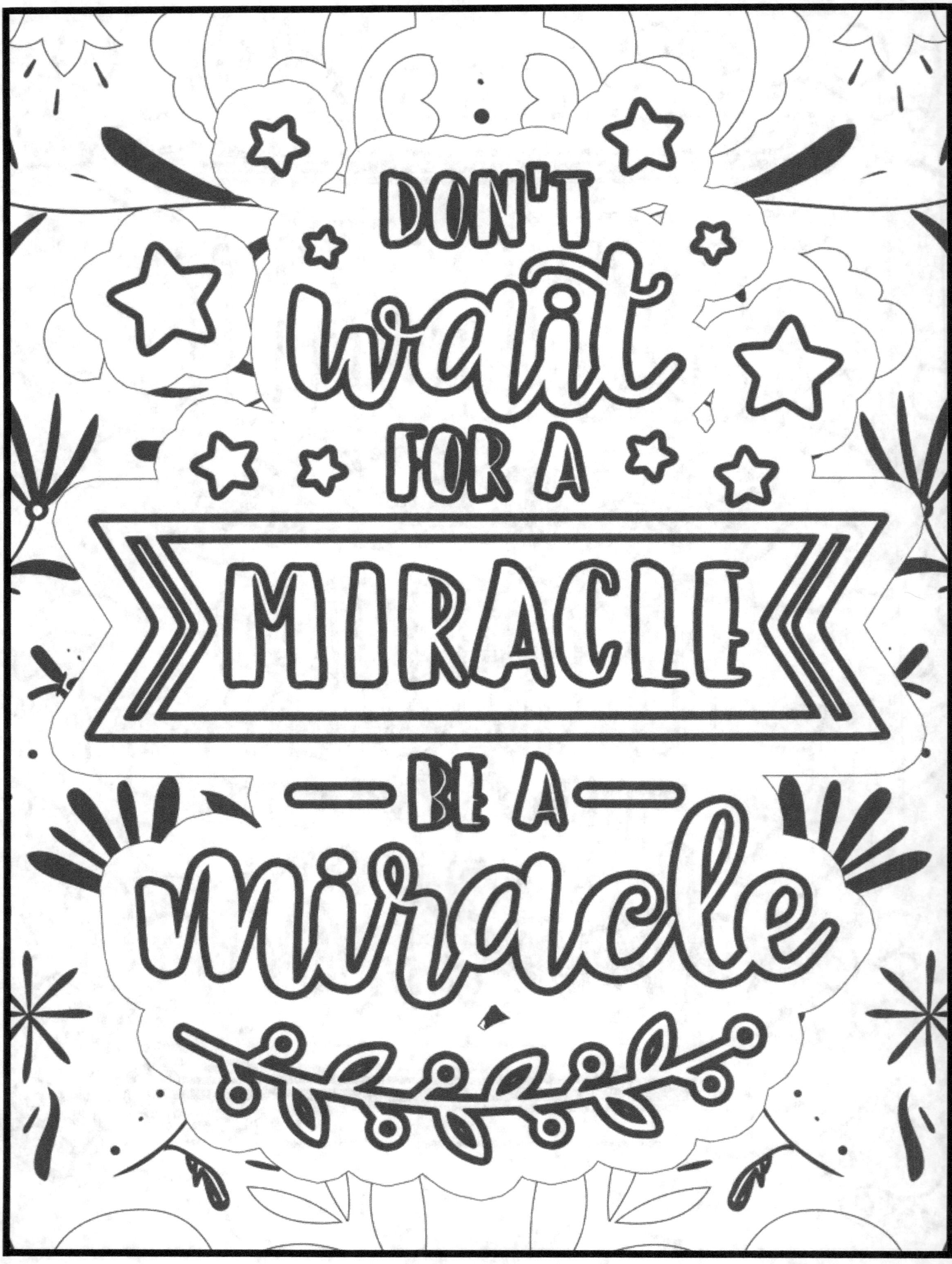
DON'T
wait
FOR A
MIRACLE
BE A
miracle

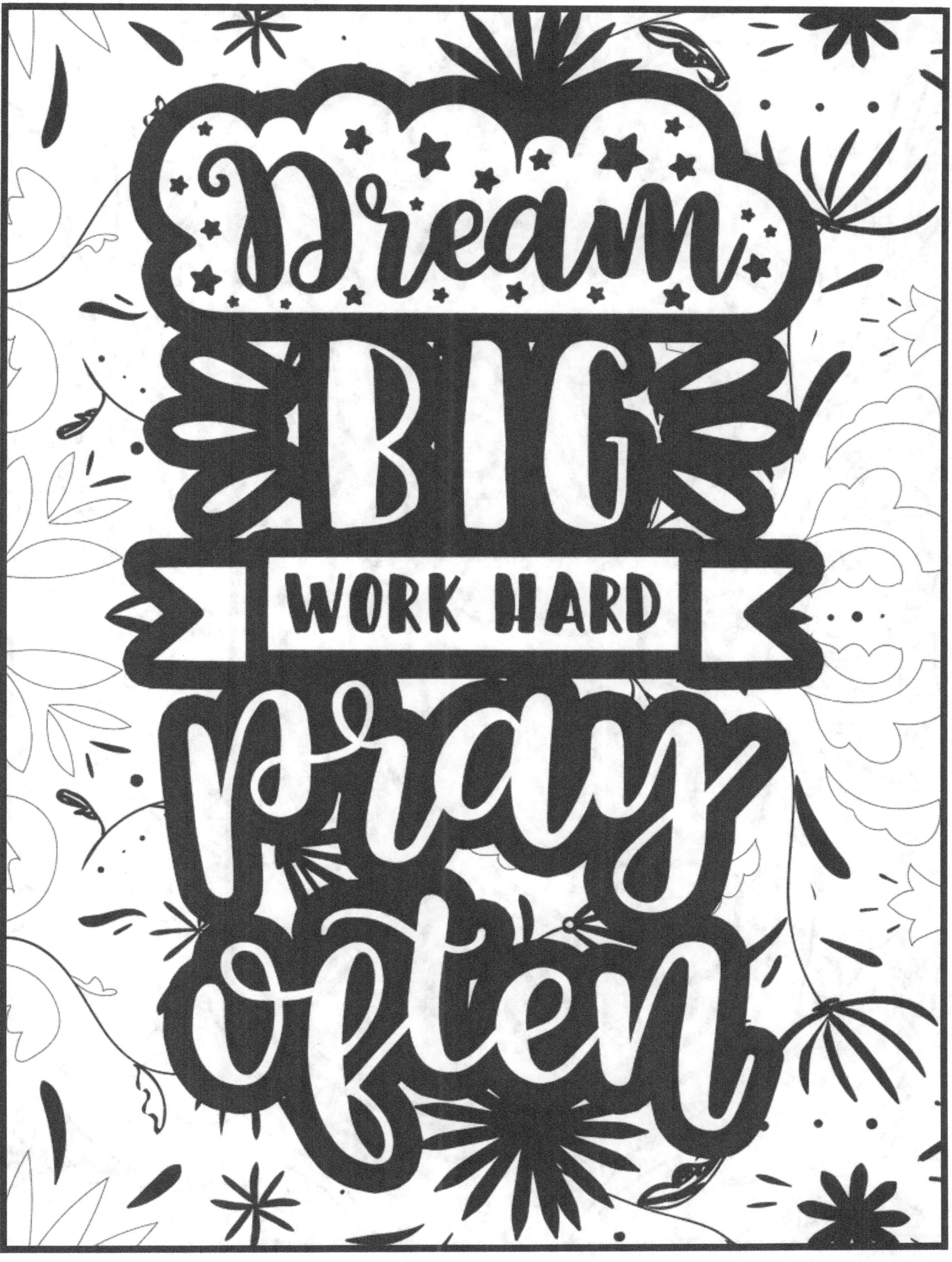
Dream
BIG
WORK HARD
pray
often

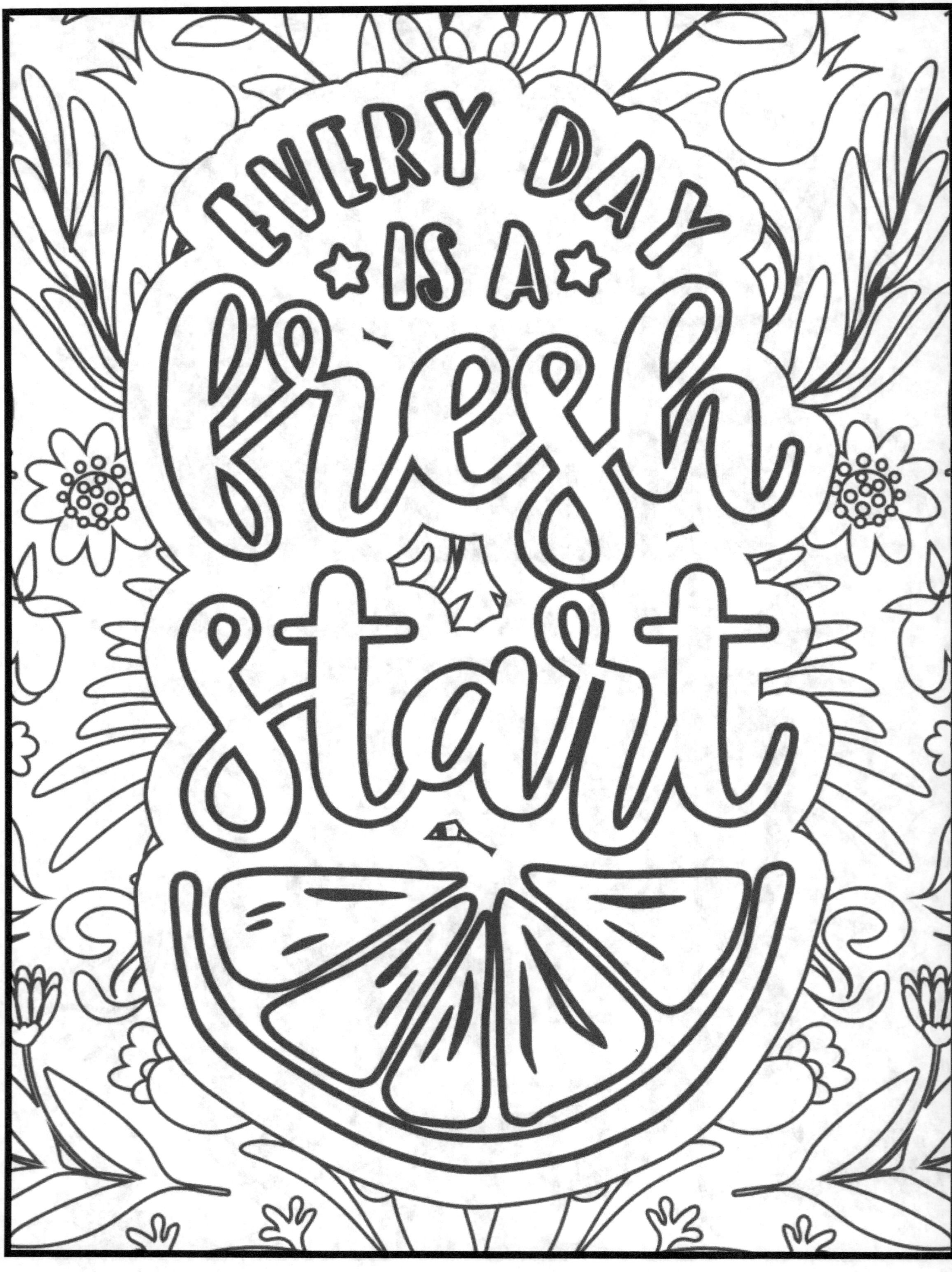
EVERY DAY
IS A
fresh
start

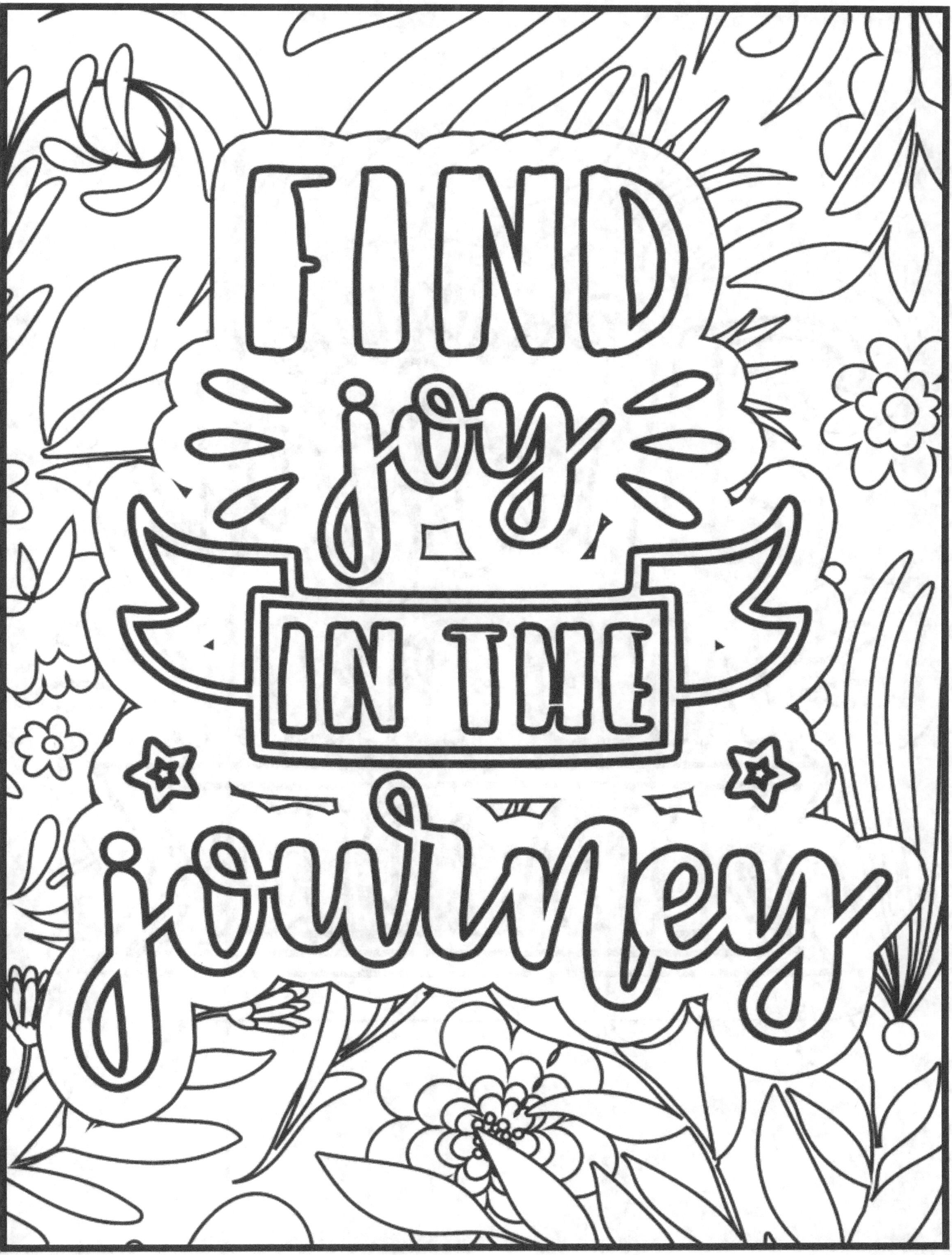
FIND
joy
IN THE
journey

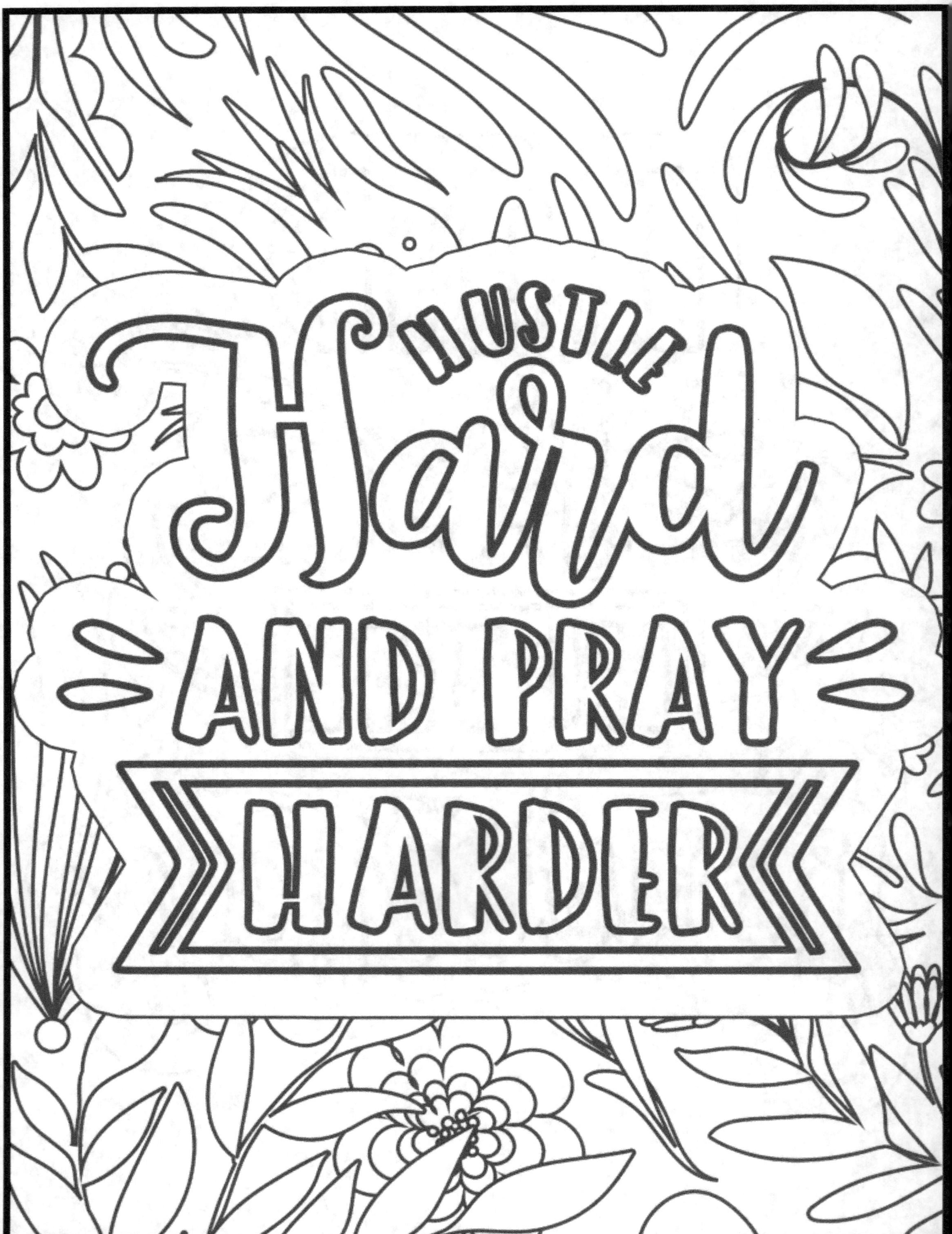
HUSTLE
Hard
AND PRAY
HARDER

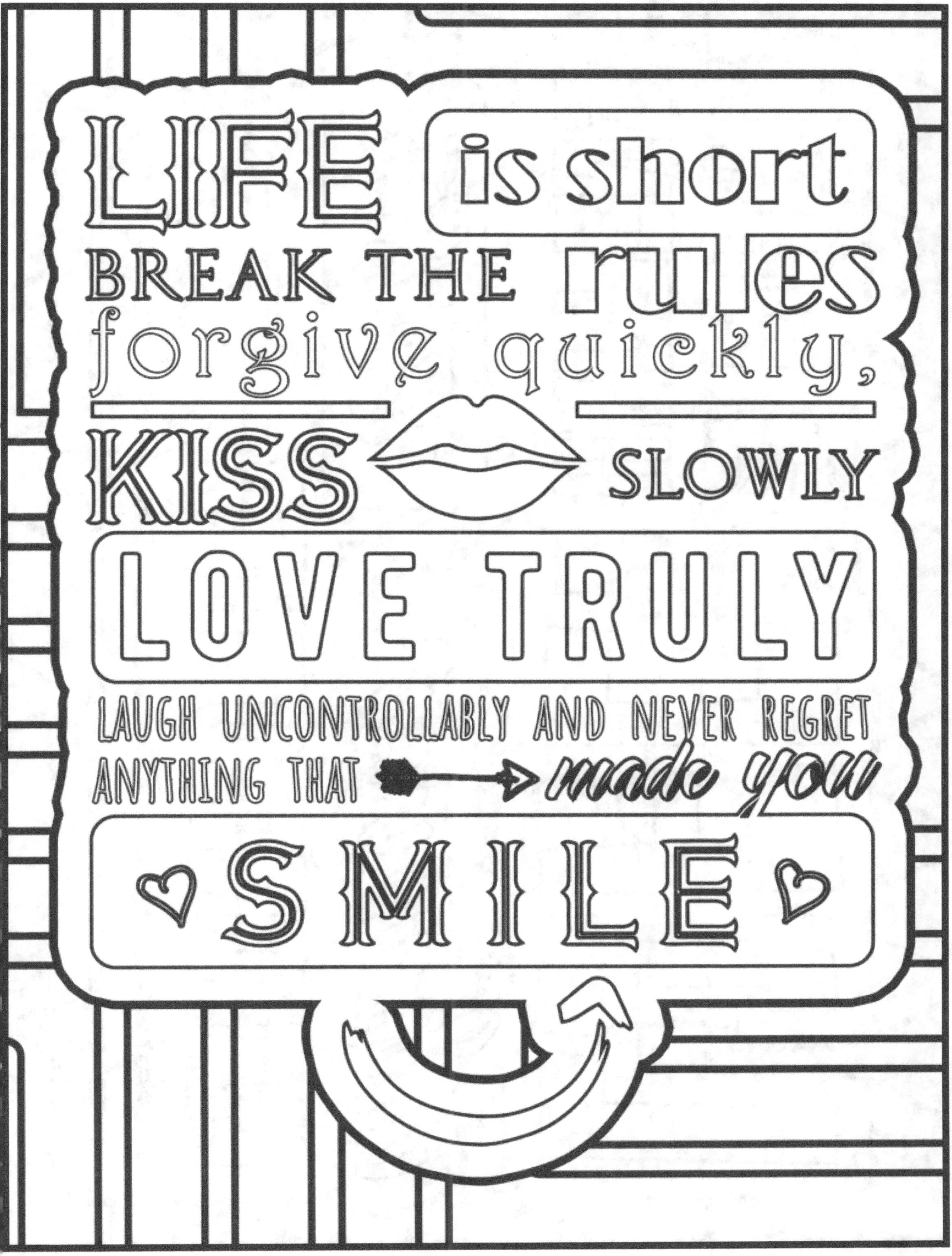
LIFE is short
BREAK THE rules
forgive quickly,
KISS SLOWLY
LOVE TRULY
LAUGH UNCONTROLLABLY AND NEVER REGRET
ANYTHING THAT made you
SMILE

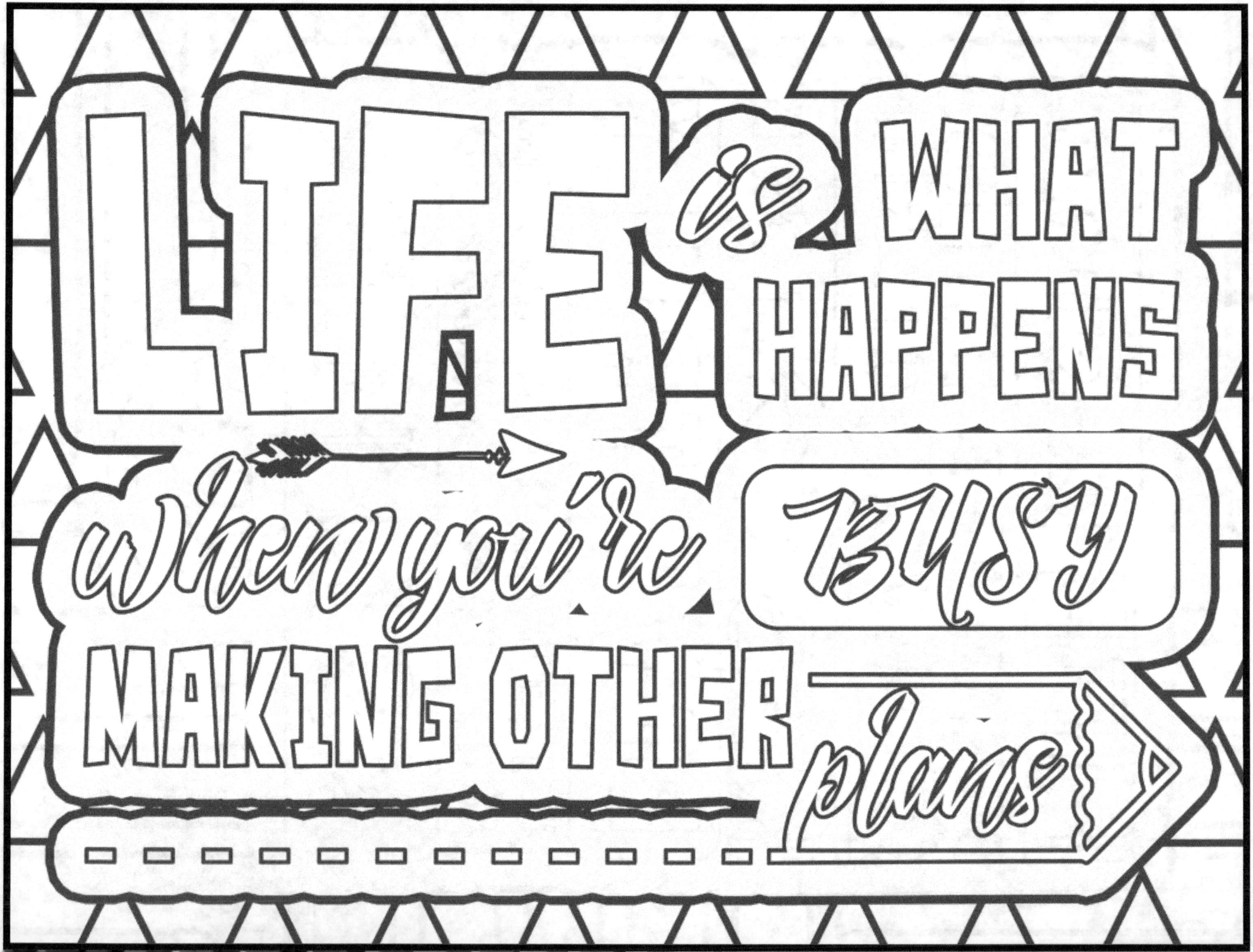
LIFE is WHAT HAPPENS
when you're BUSY
MAKING OTHER plans

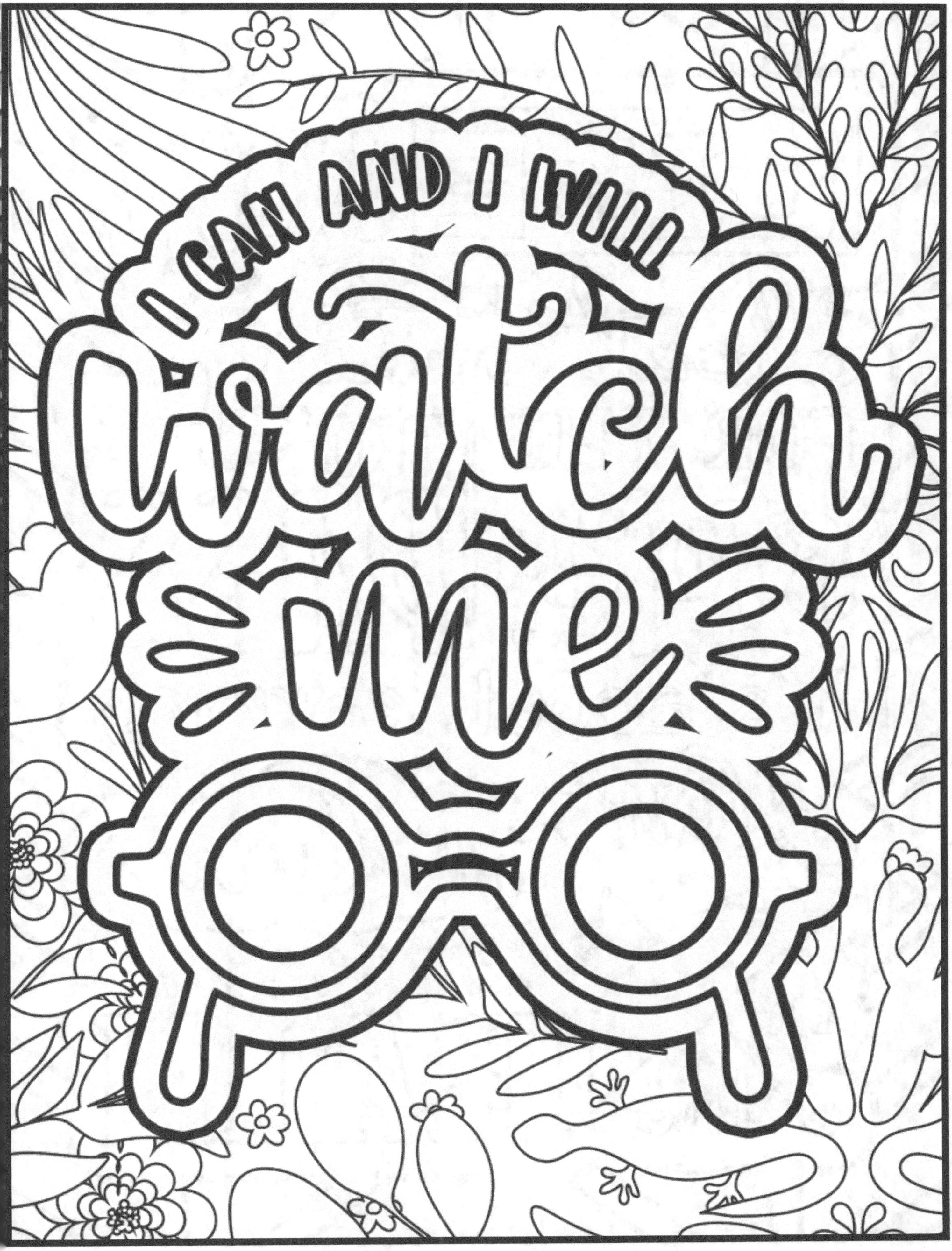
I CAN AND I WILL
watch
me

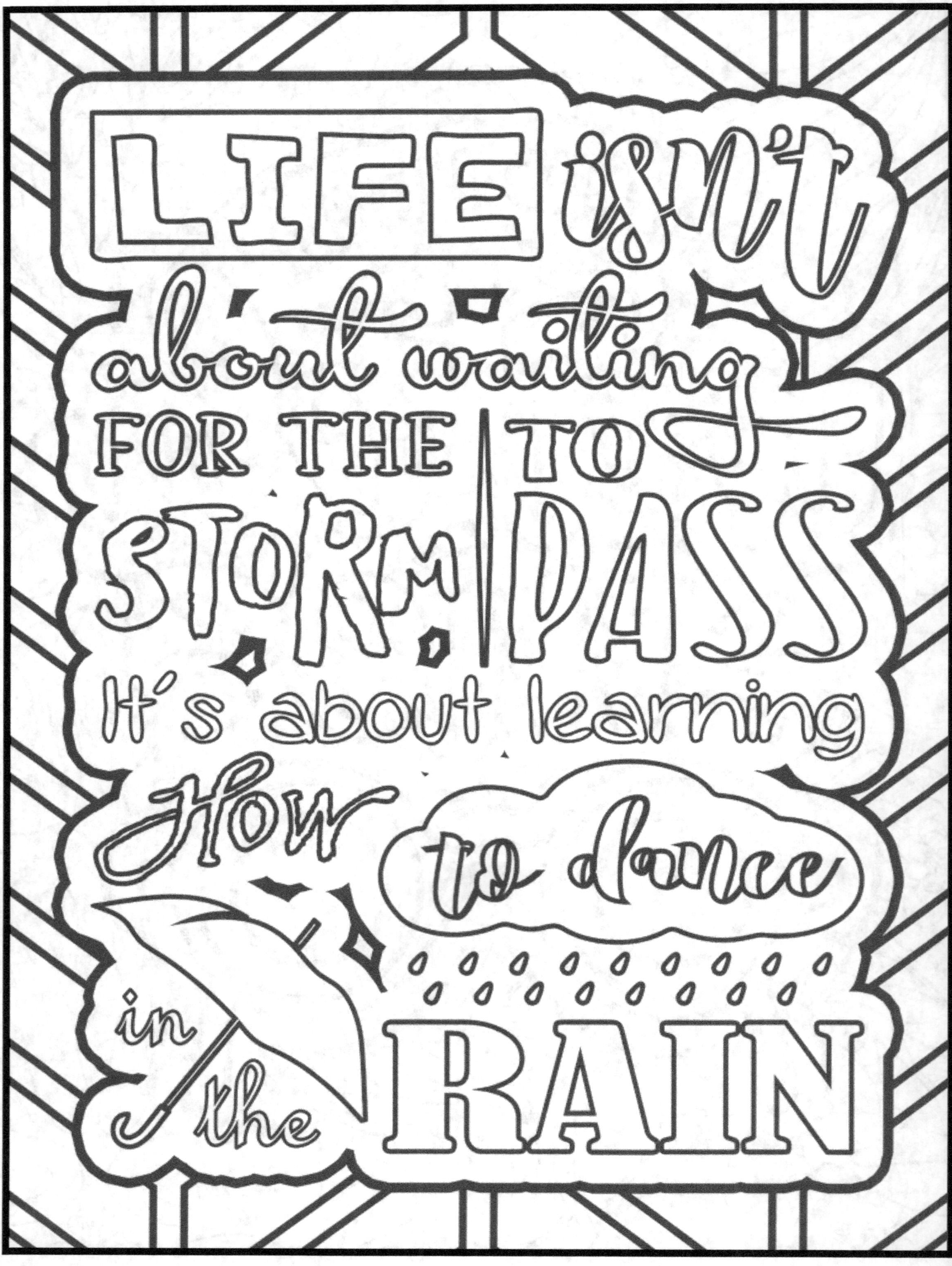
LIFE isn't
about waiting
FOR THE
STORM
TO
PASS
It's about learning
How
to dance
in
the
RAIN

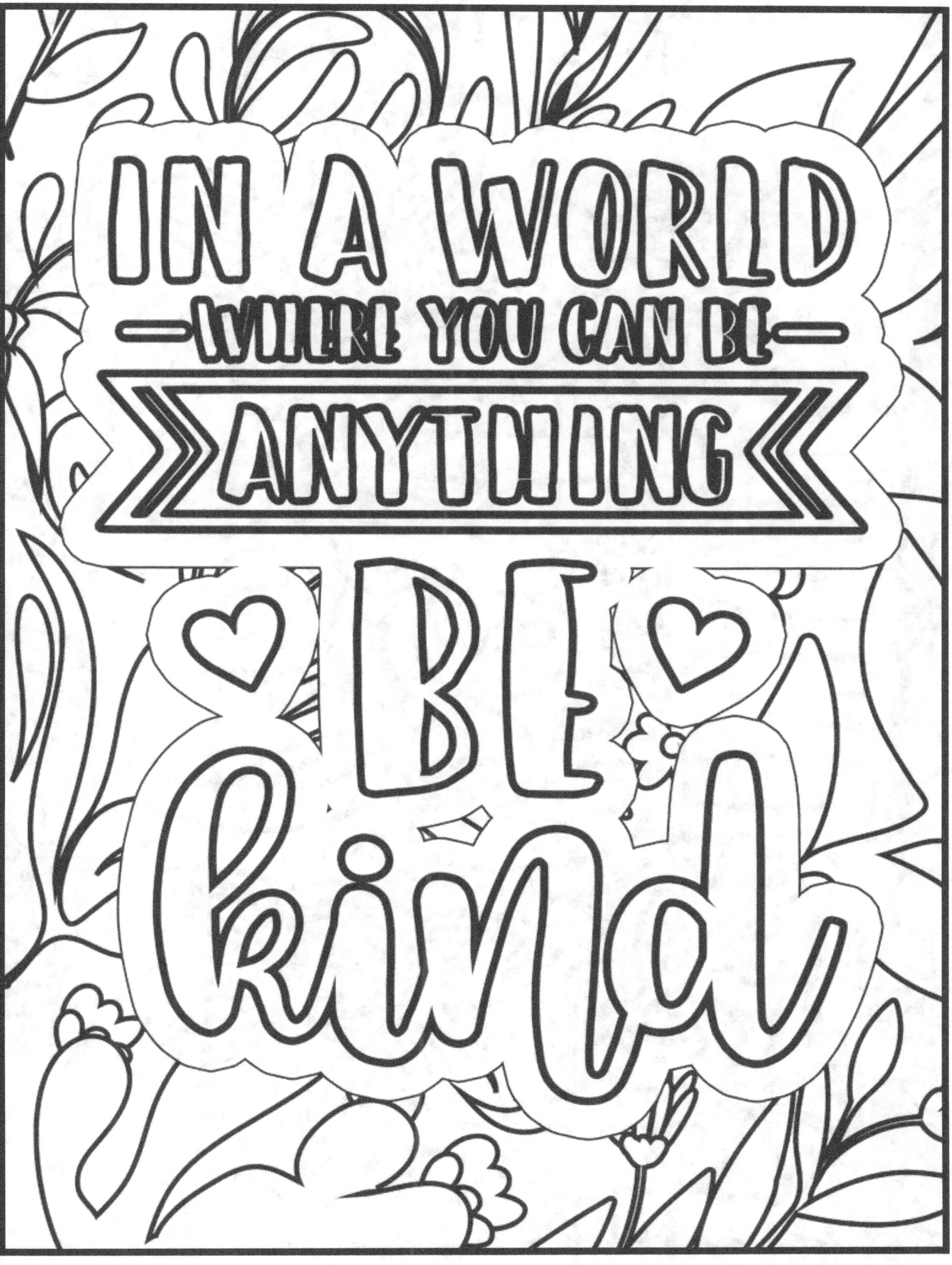
IN A WORLD
WHERE YOU CAN BE
ANYTHING
BE
kind

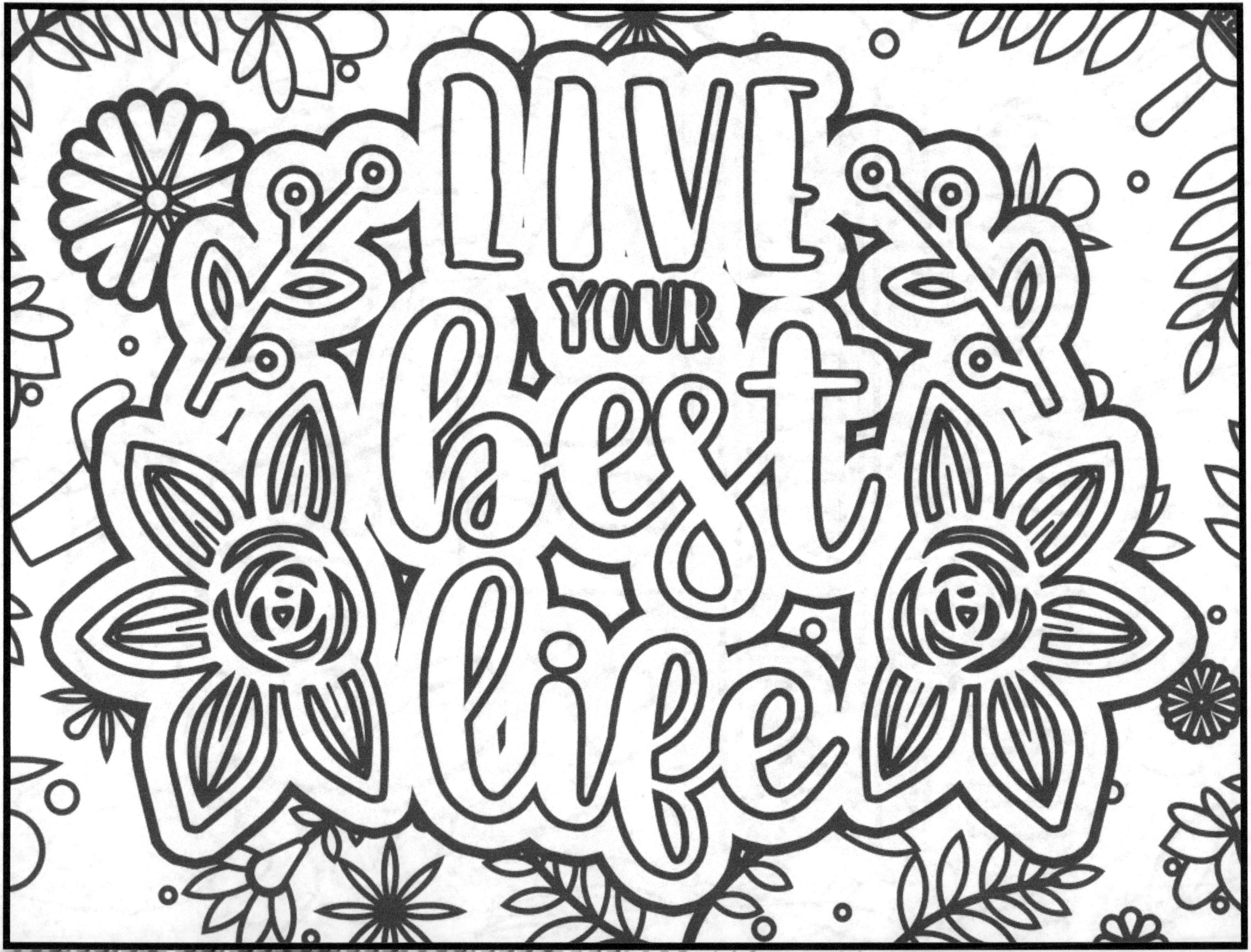
LIVE
YOUR
best
life

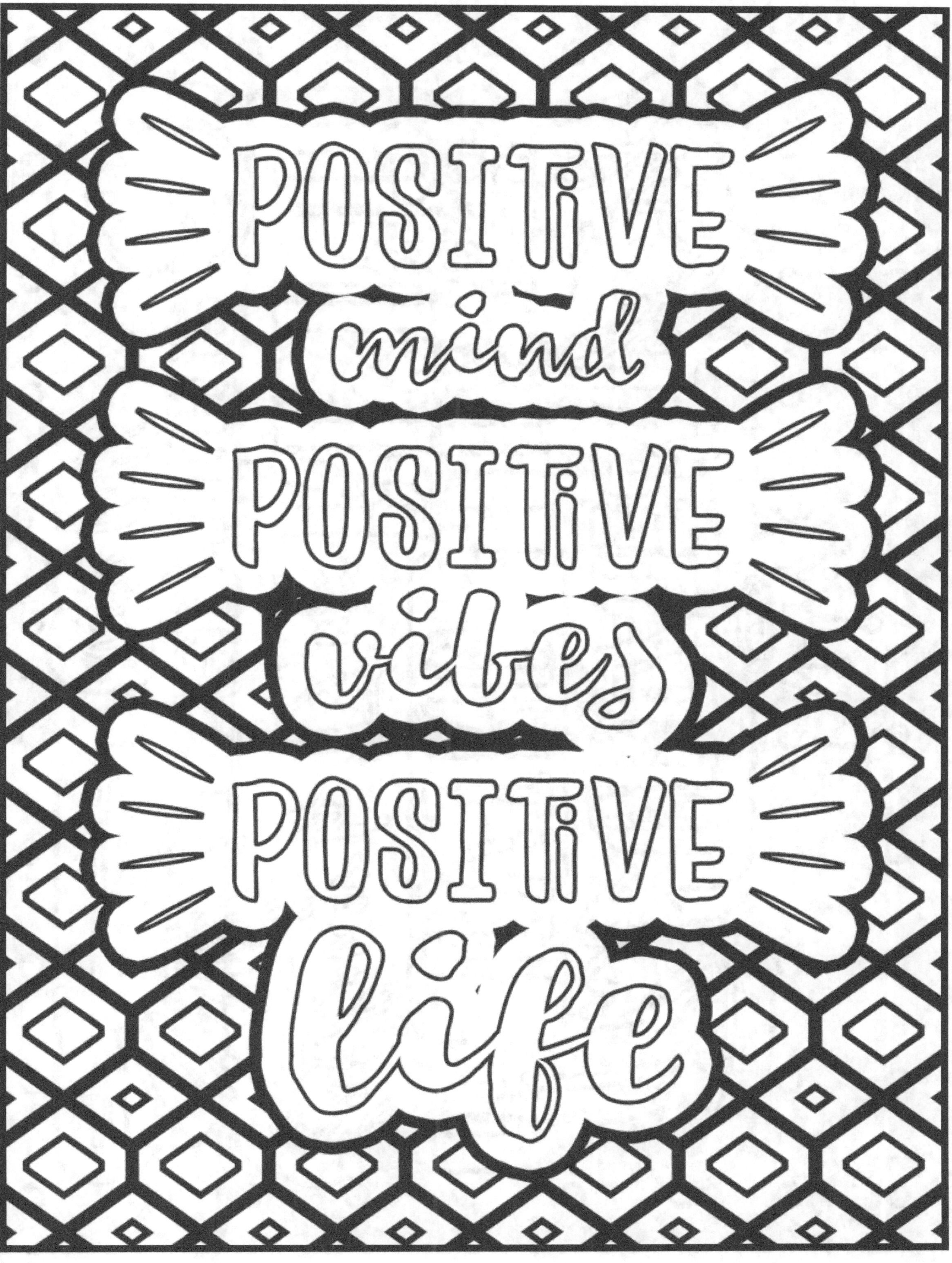
POSITIVE
mind
POSITIVE
vibes
POSITIVE
life

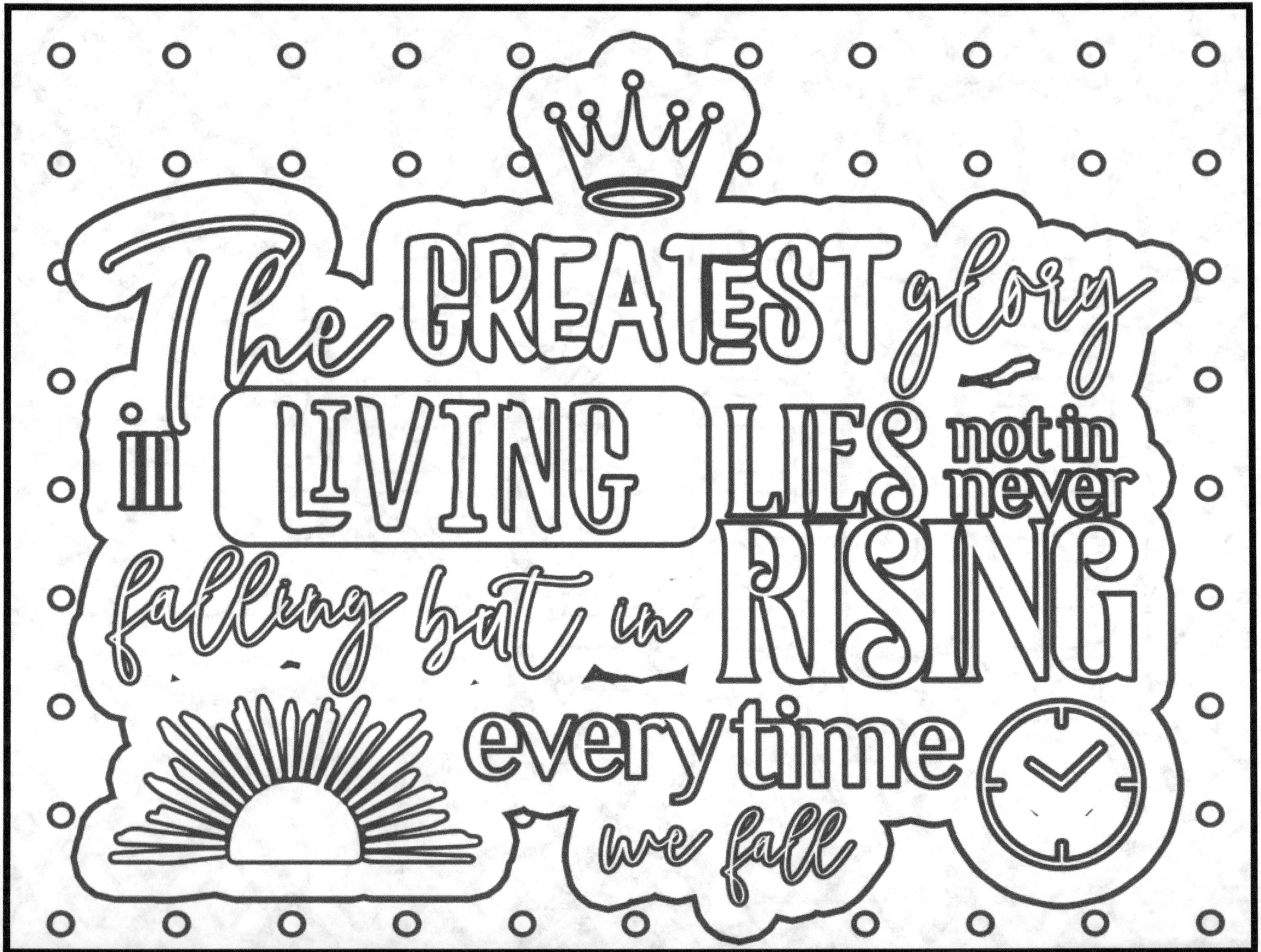

The GREATEST glory
in LIVING LIES not in never
falling but in RISING
every time
we fall

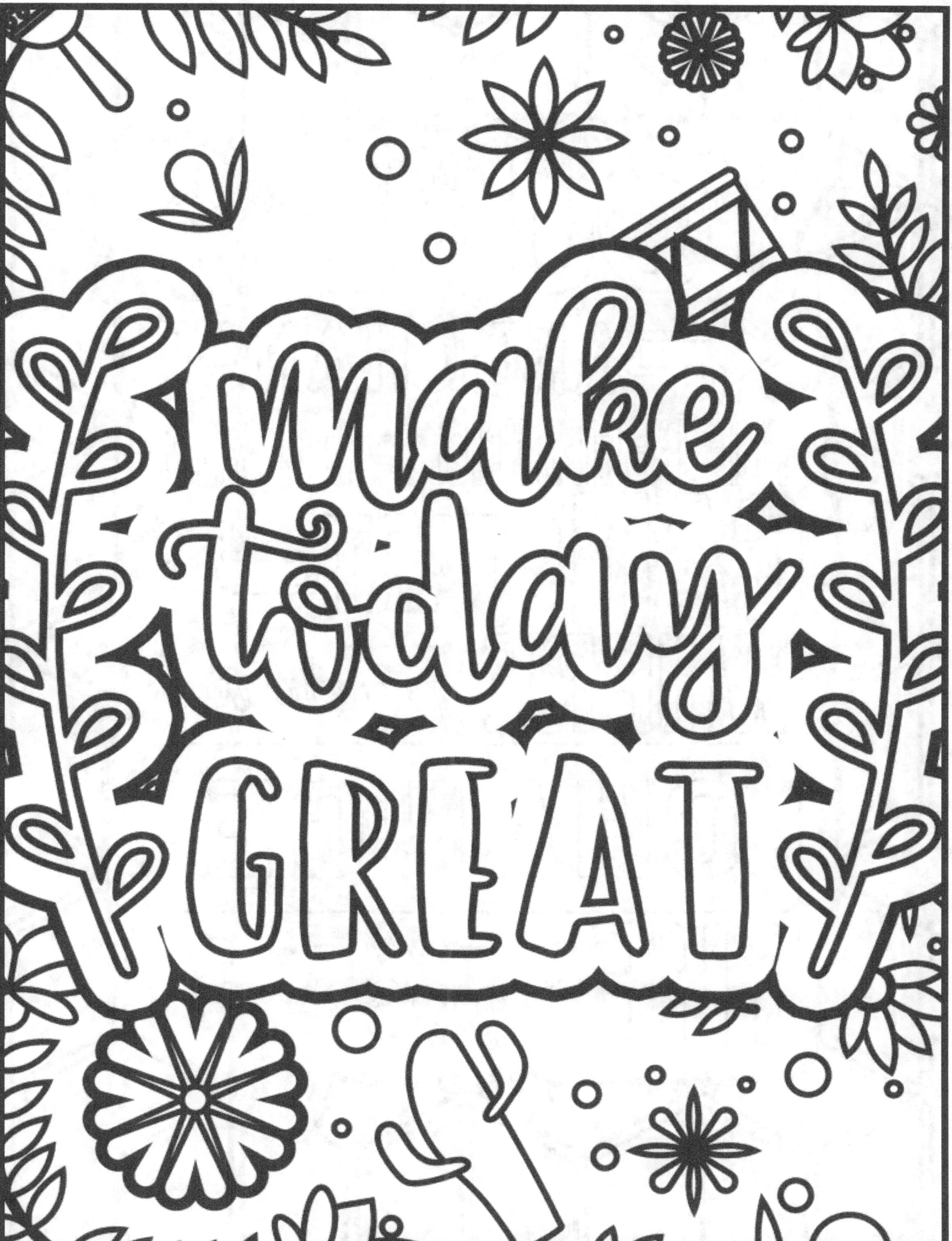
make today GREAT

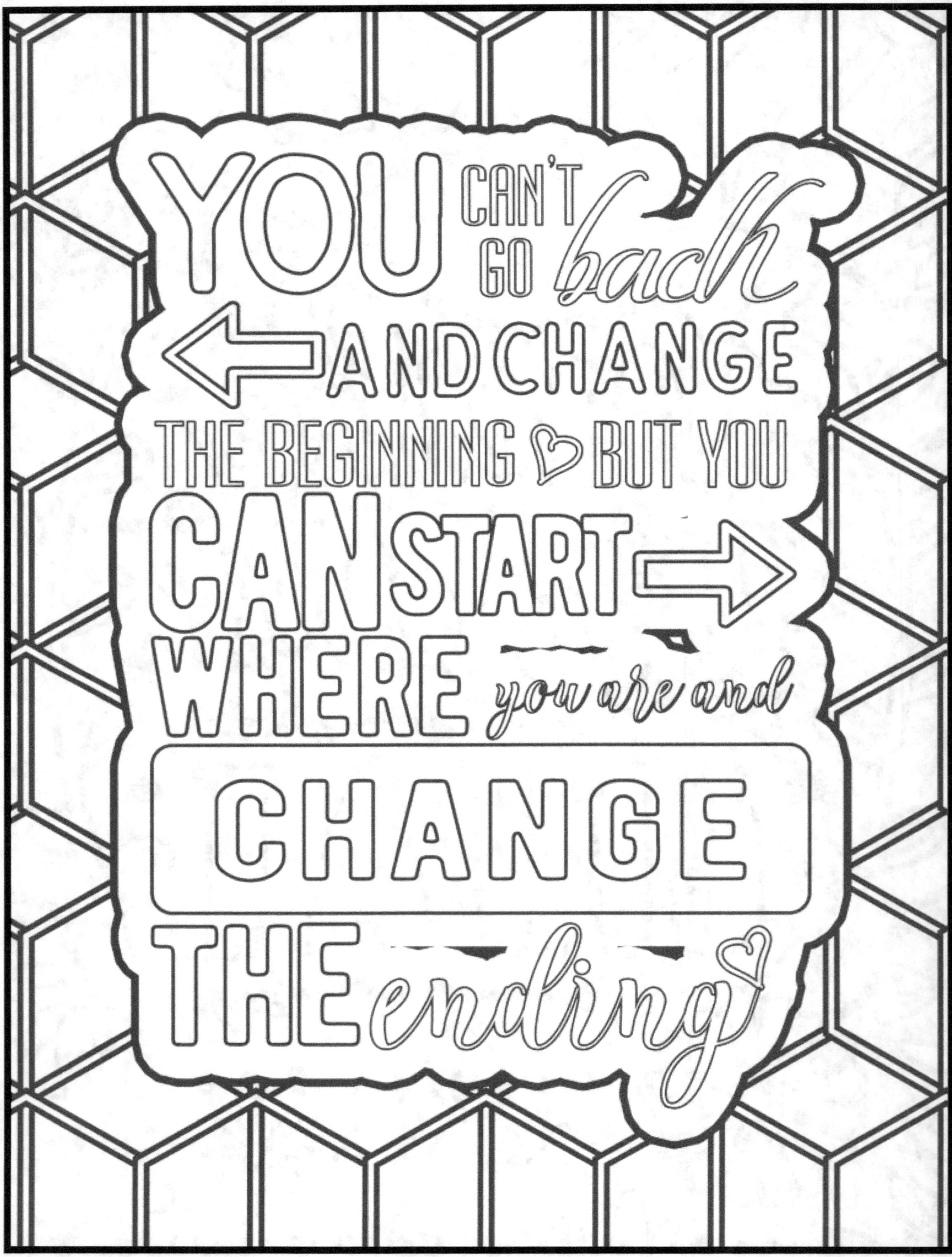
YOU CAN'T GO back
AND CHANGE
THE BEGINNING BUT YOU
CAN START
WHERE you are and
CHANGE
THE ending

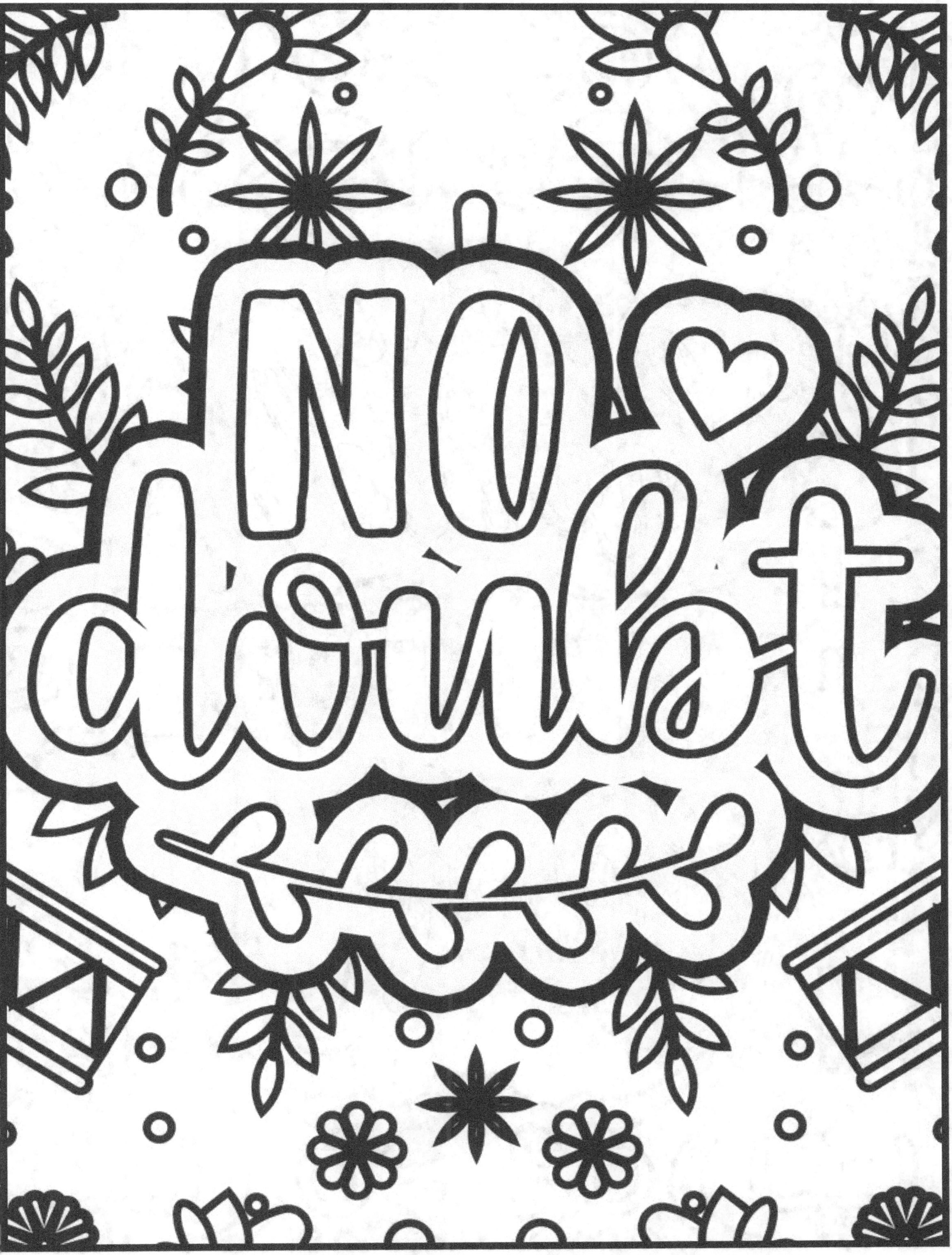
NO
doubt

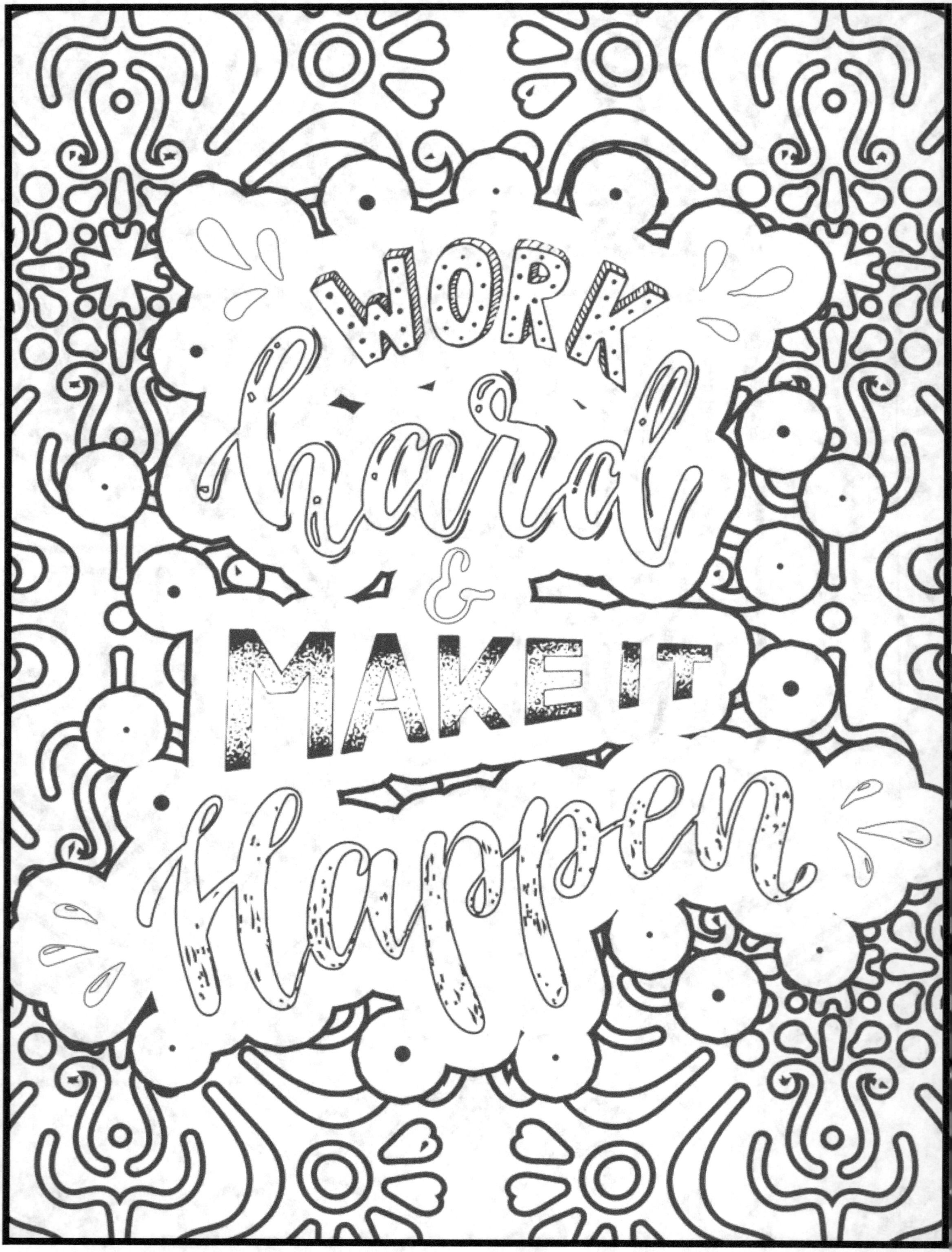
WORK
hard
&
MAKE IT
Happen

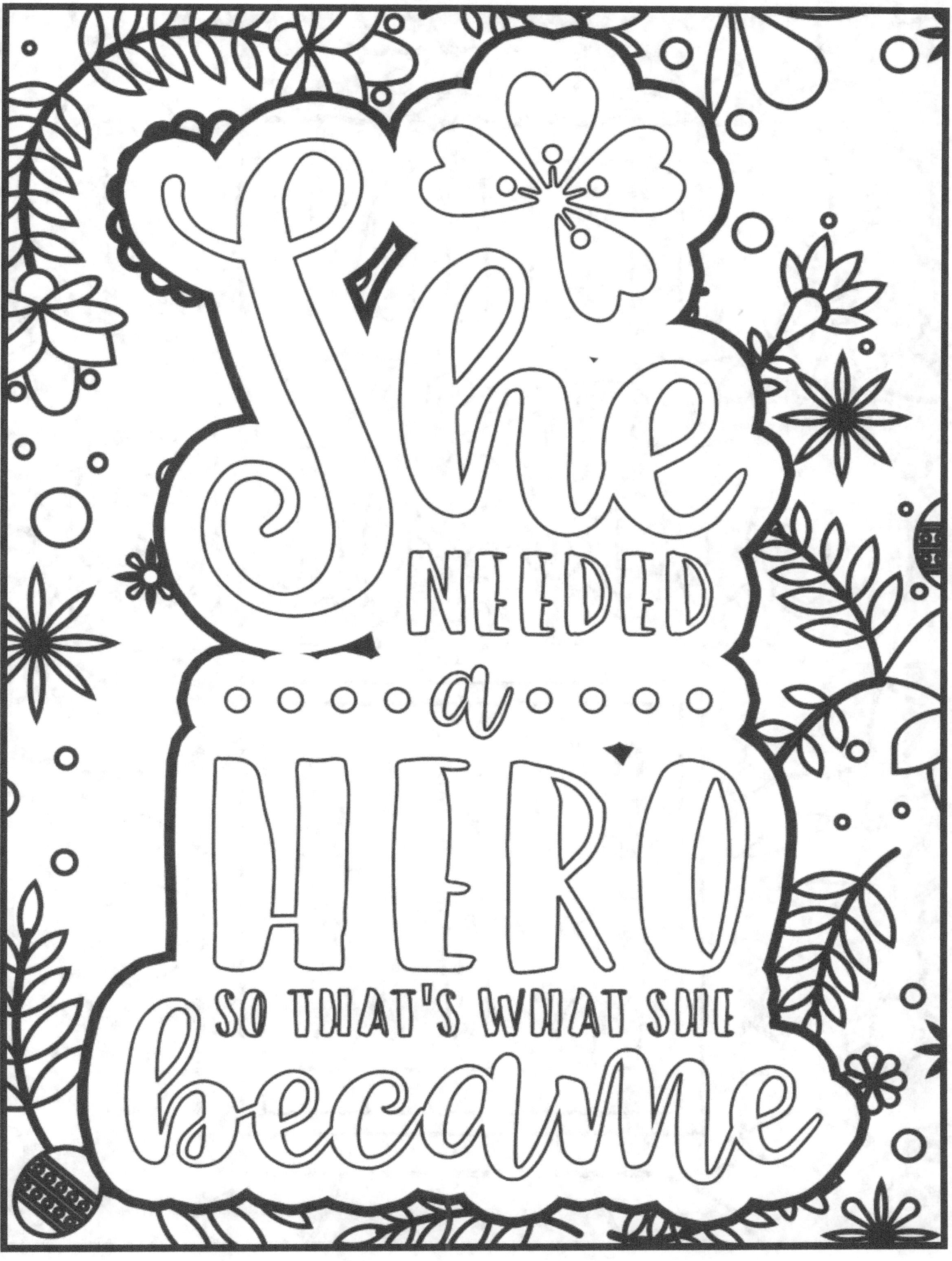
She
NEEDED
a
HERO
SO THAT'S WHAT SHE
became

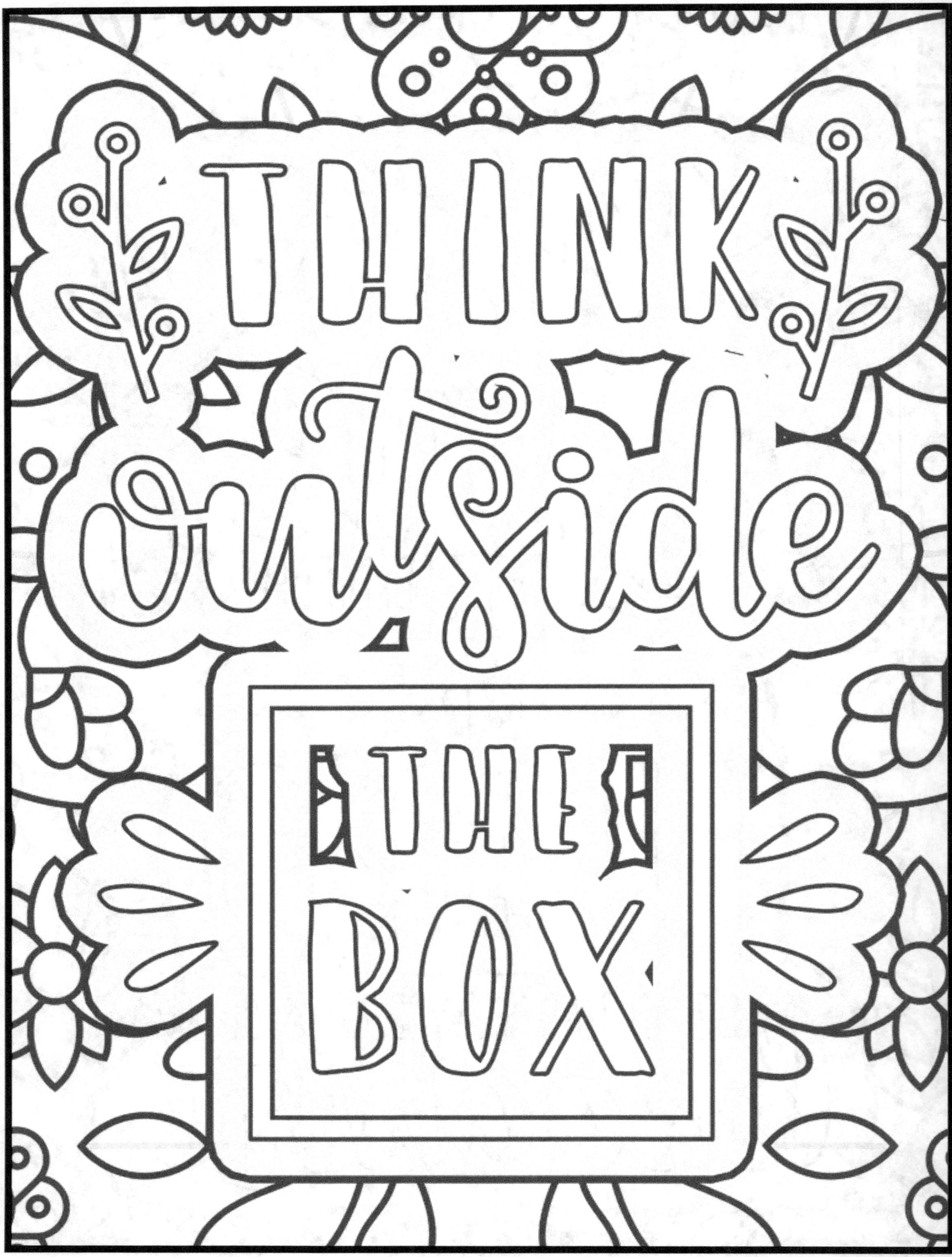
THINK
outside
THE
BOX

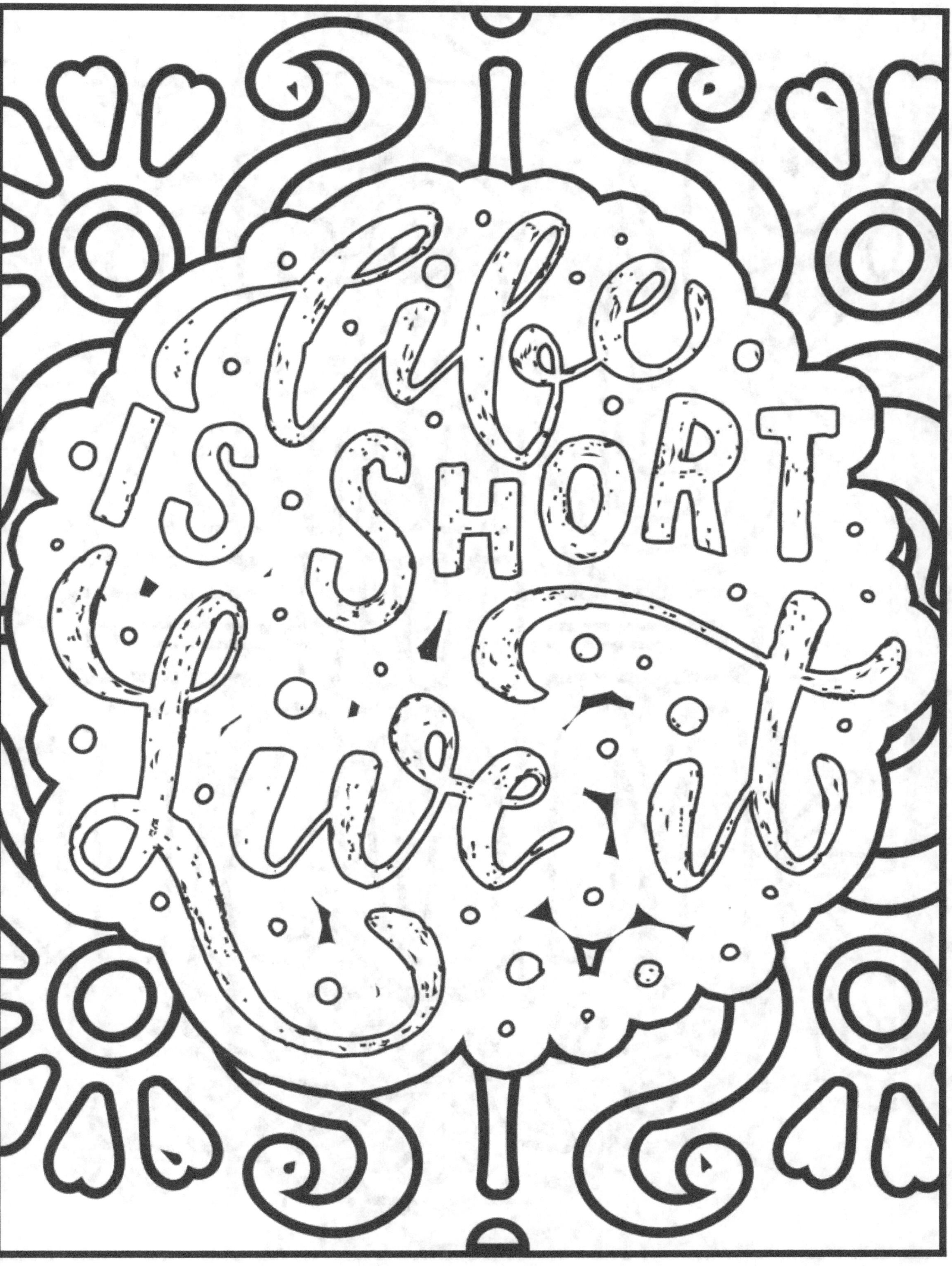
Life
IS SHORT
Live it

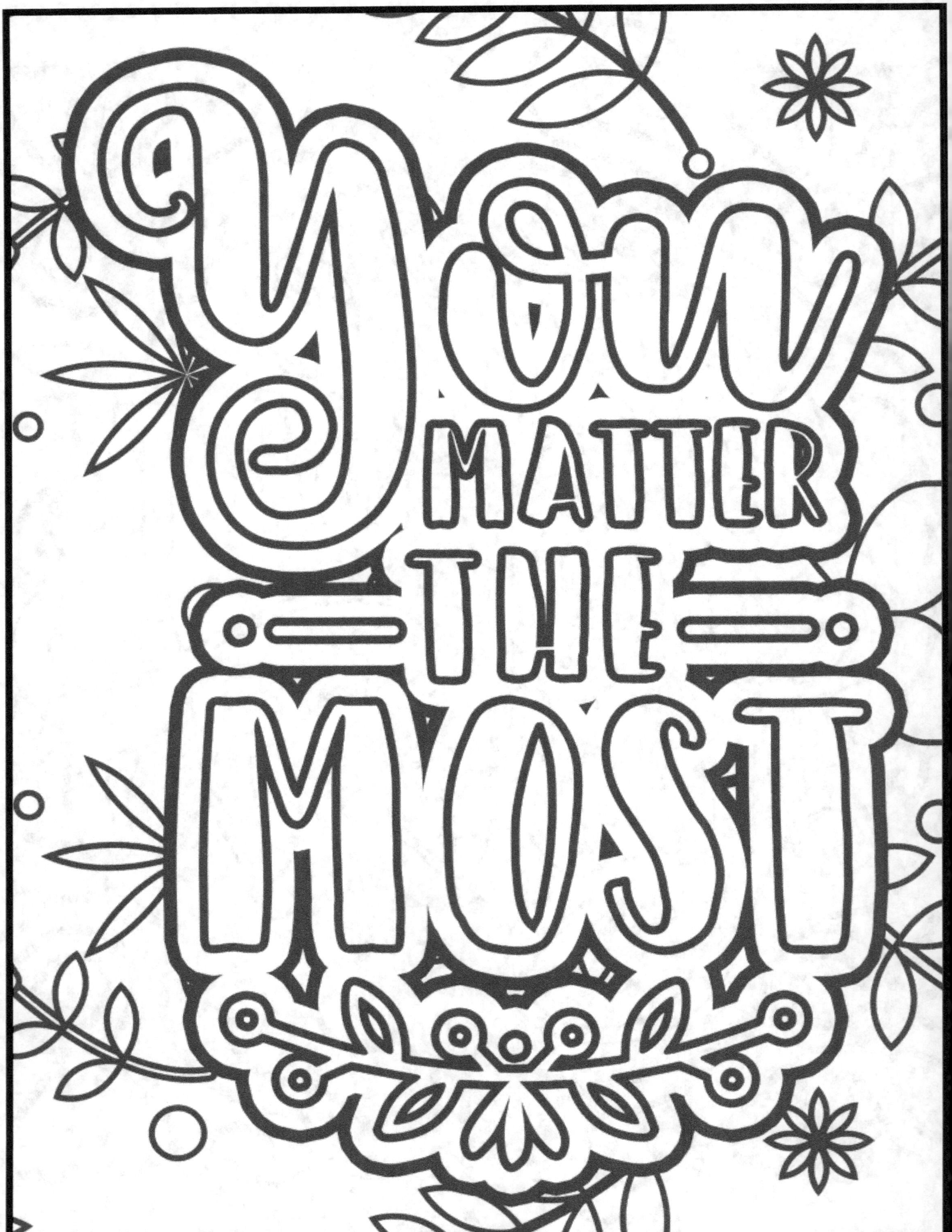
You
MATTER
THE
MOST

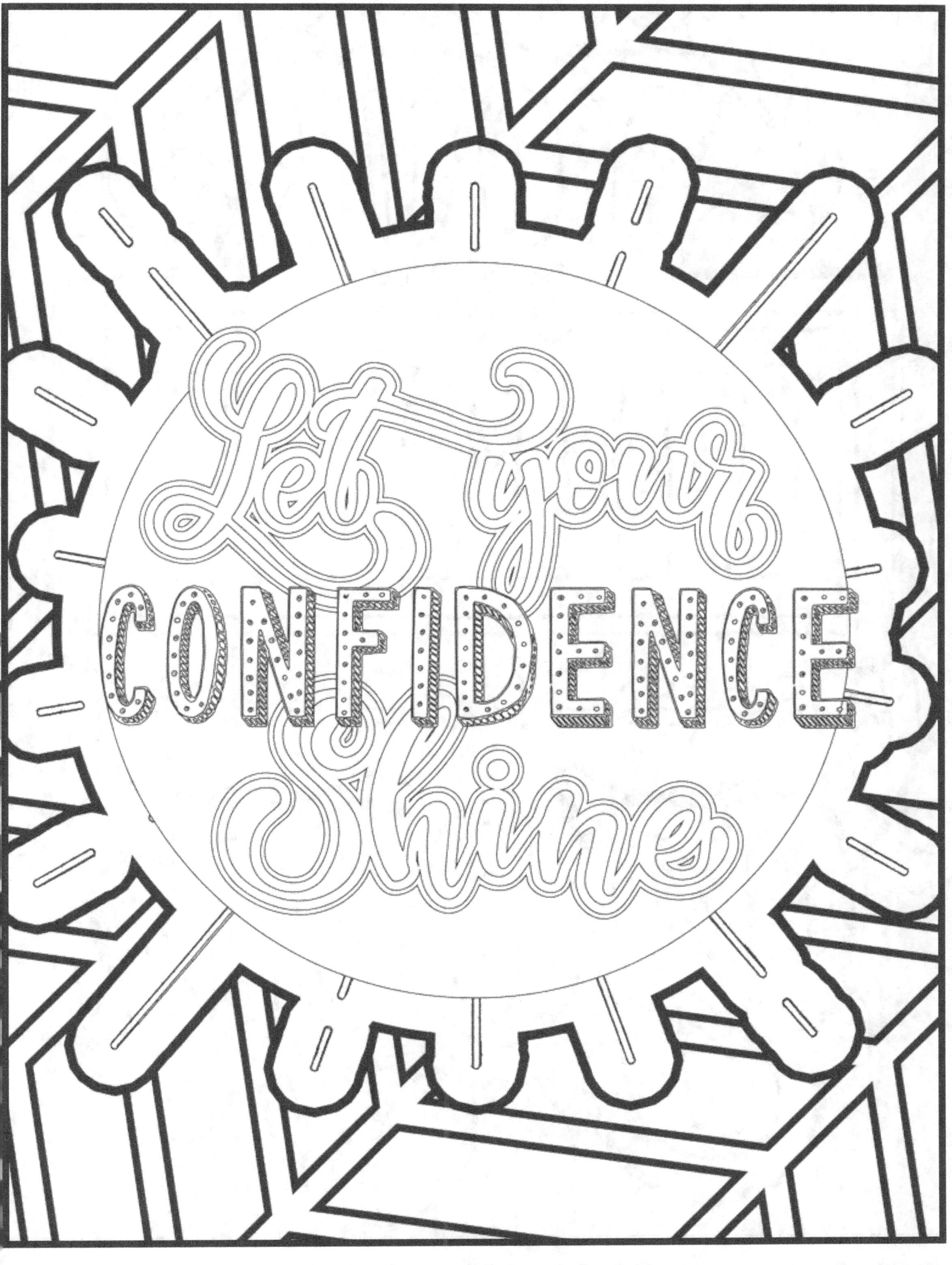
Let your
CONFIDENCE
Shine

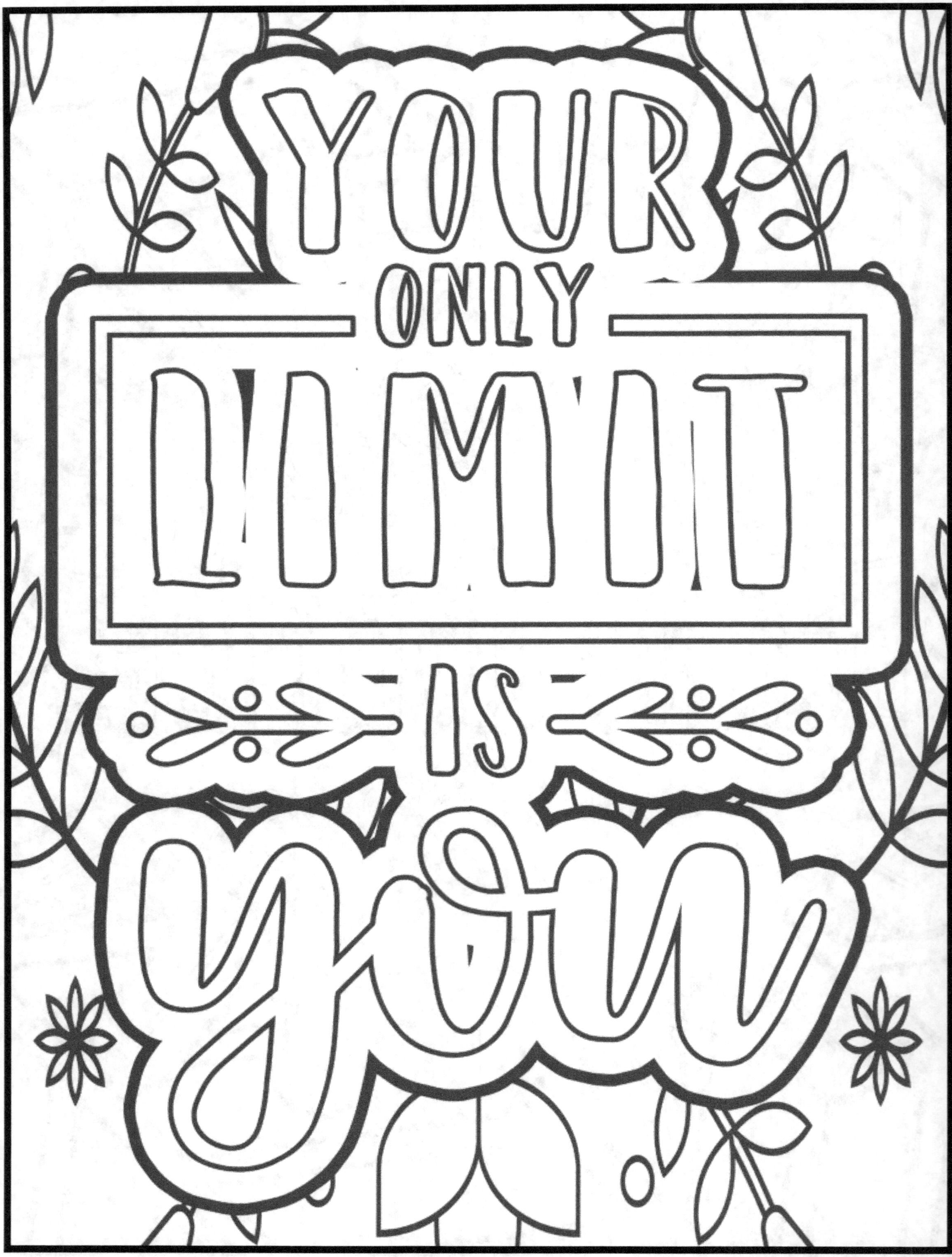
YOUR
ONLY
LIMIT
IS
you

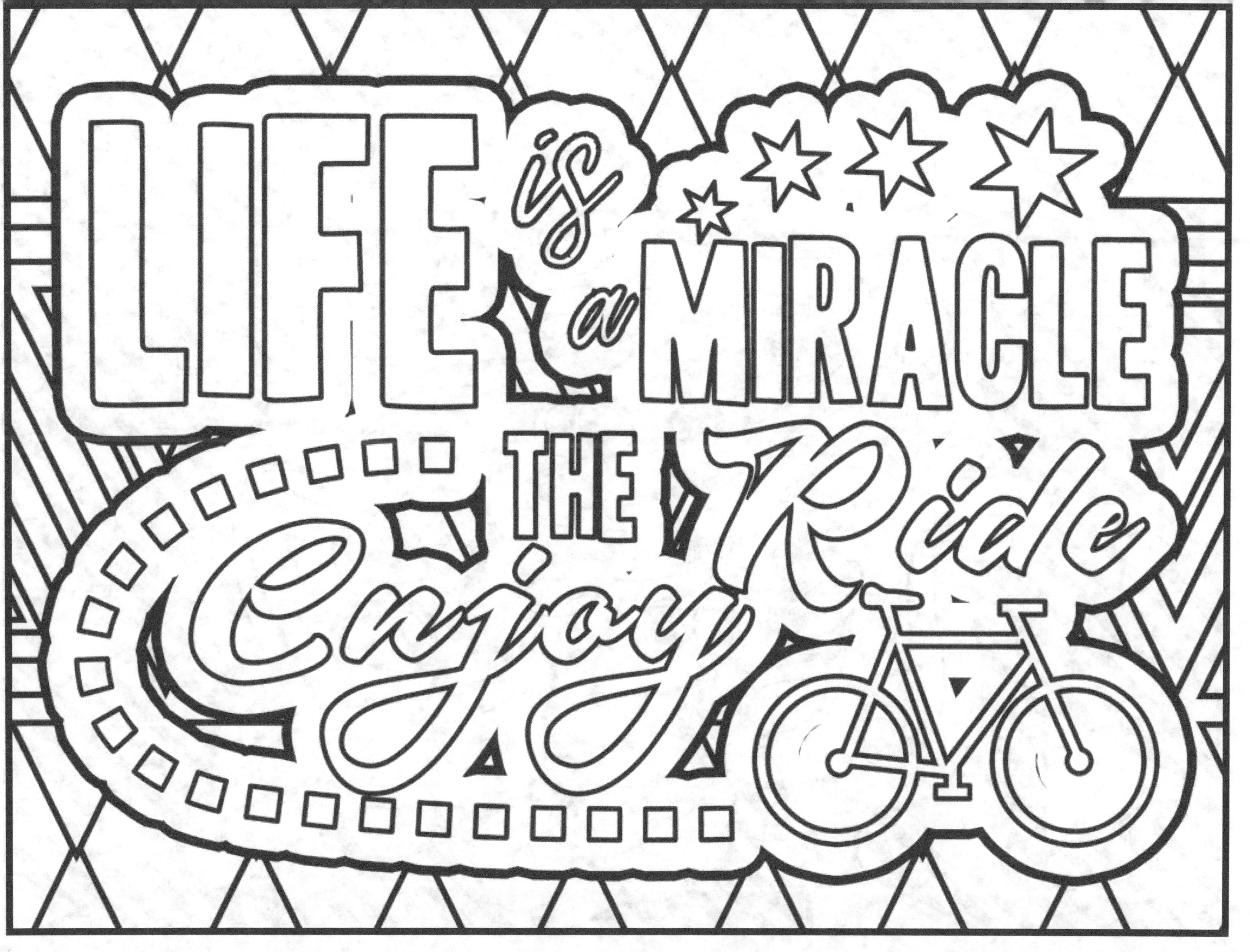
LIFE is a MIRACLE
Enjoy THE Ride

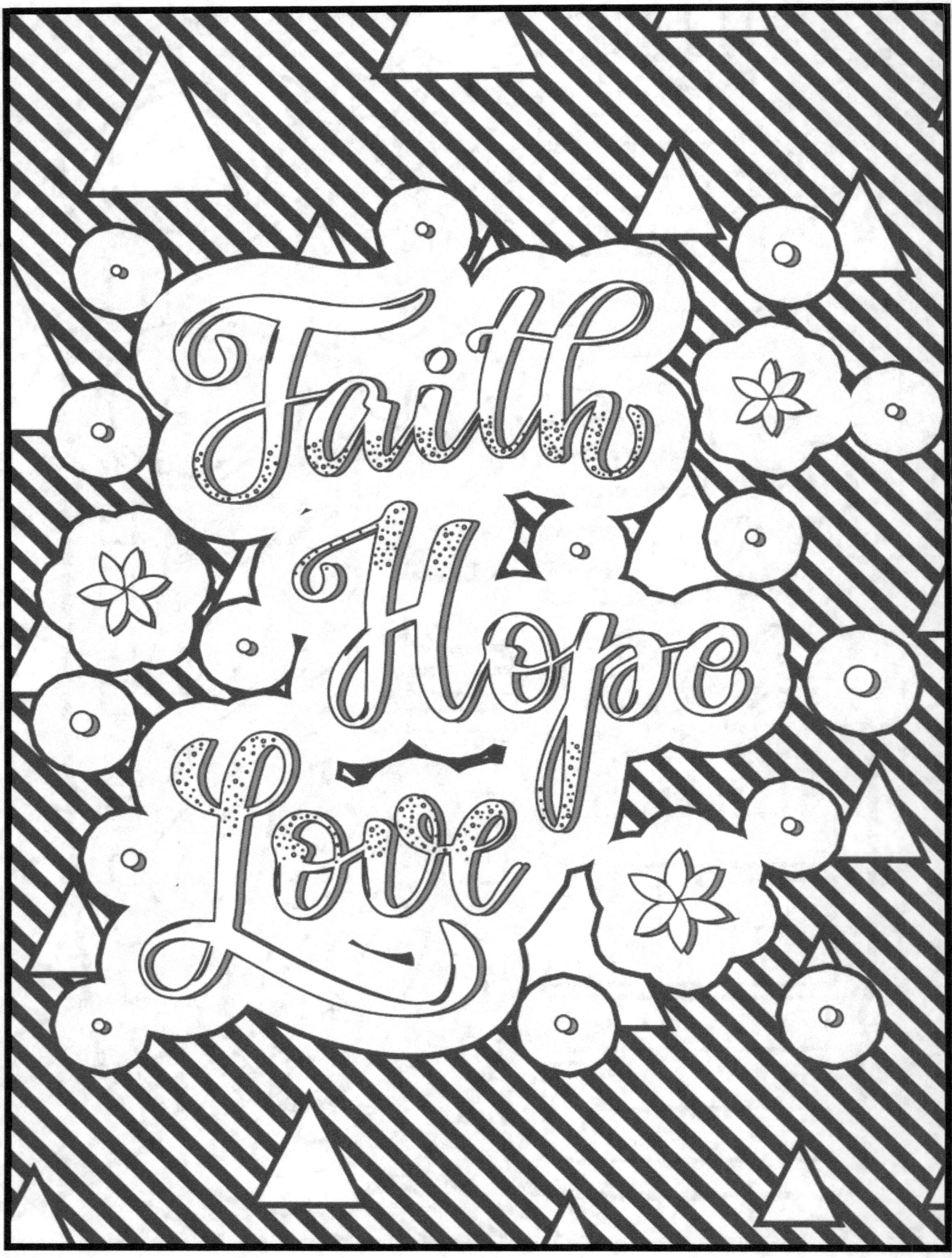
Faith
Hope
Love

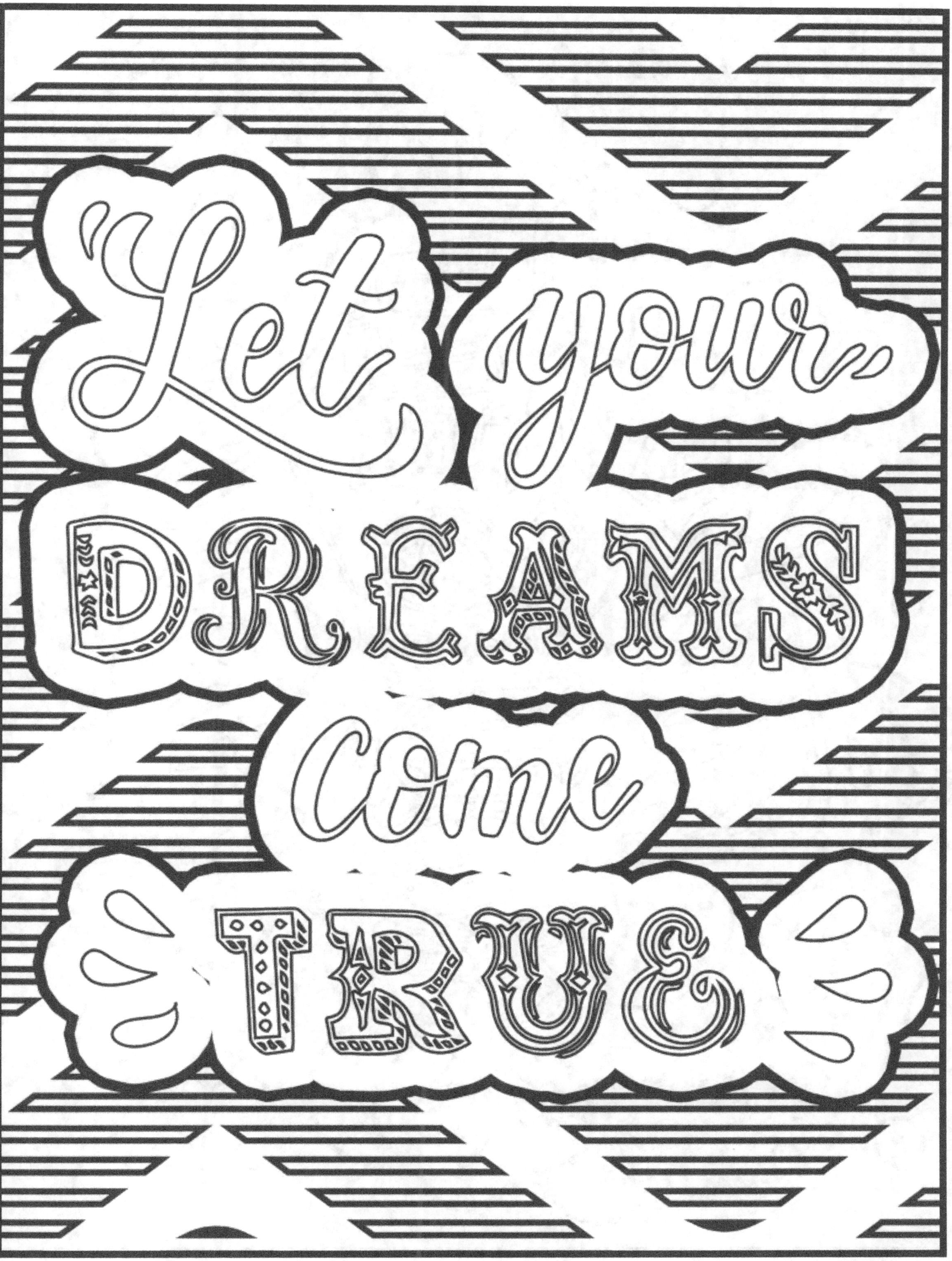
Let your
DREAMS
Come
TRUE

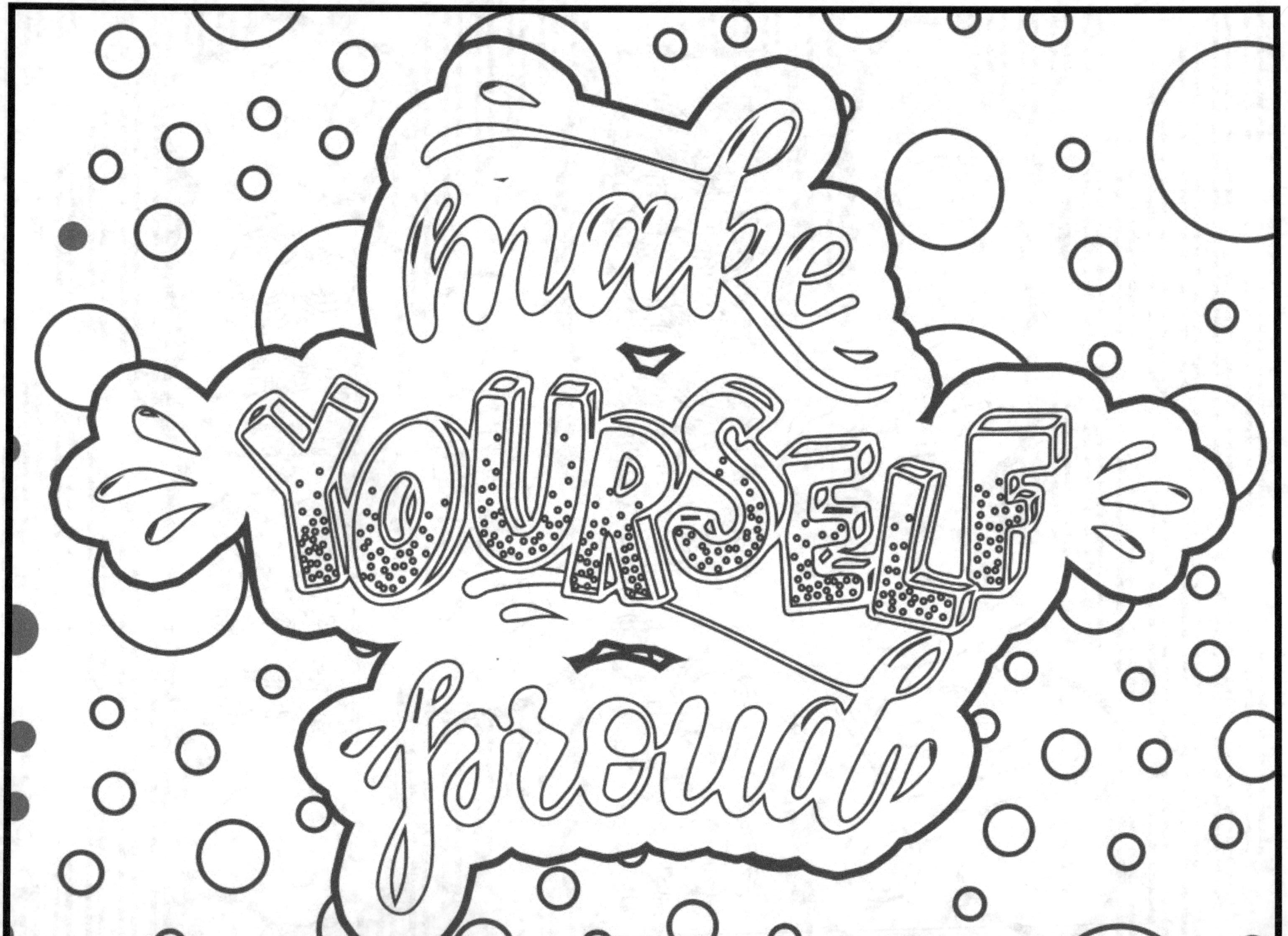
make
YOURSELF
proud

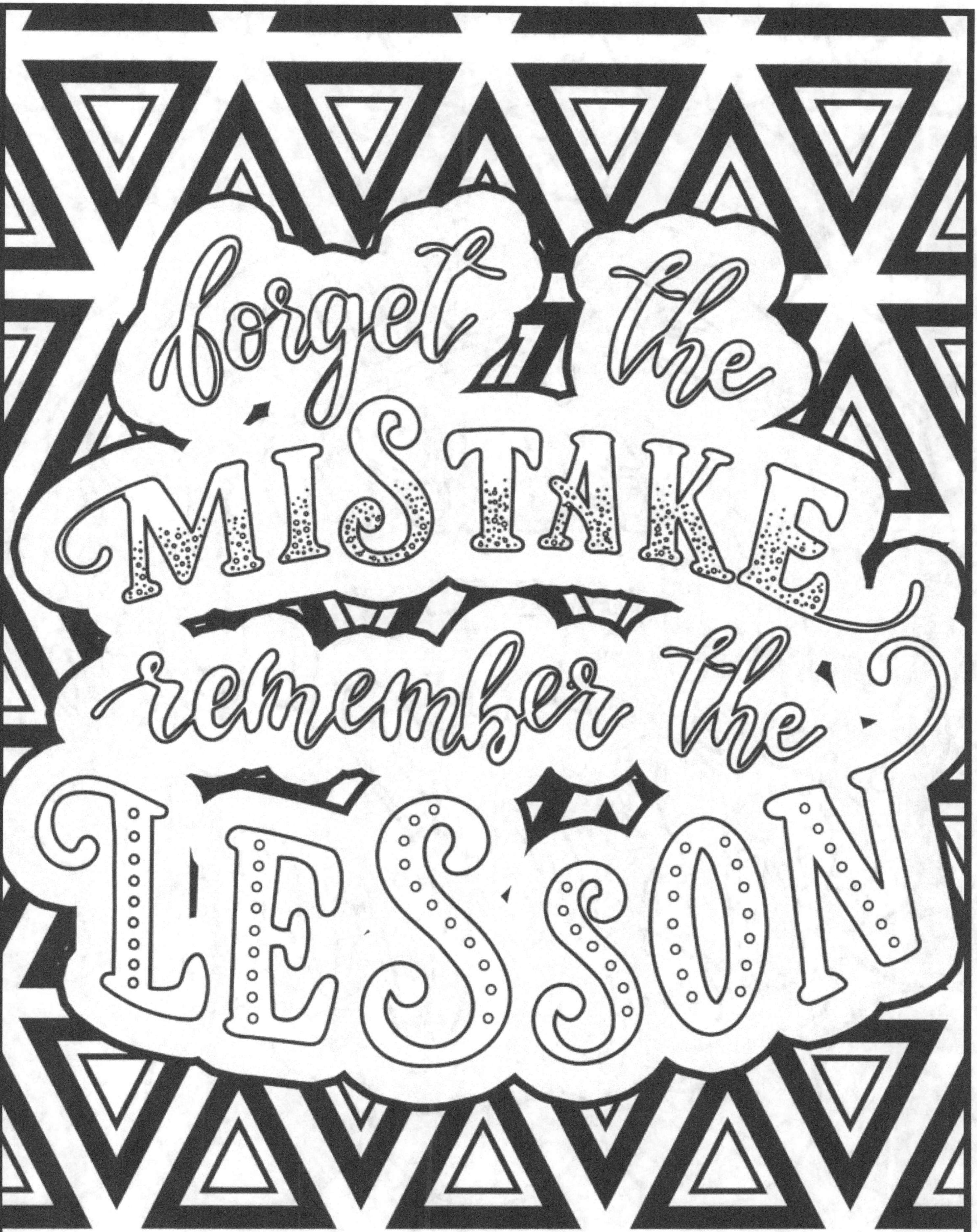
forget the
MISTAKE
remember the
LESSON

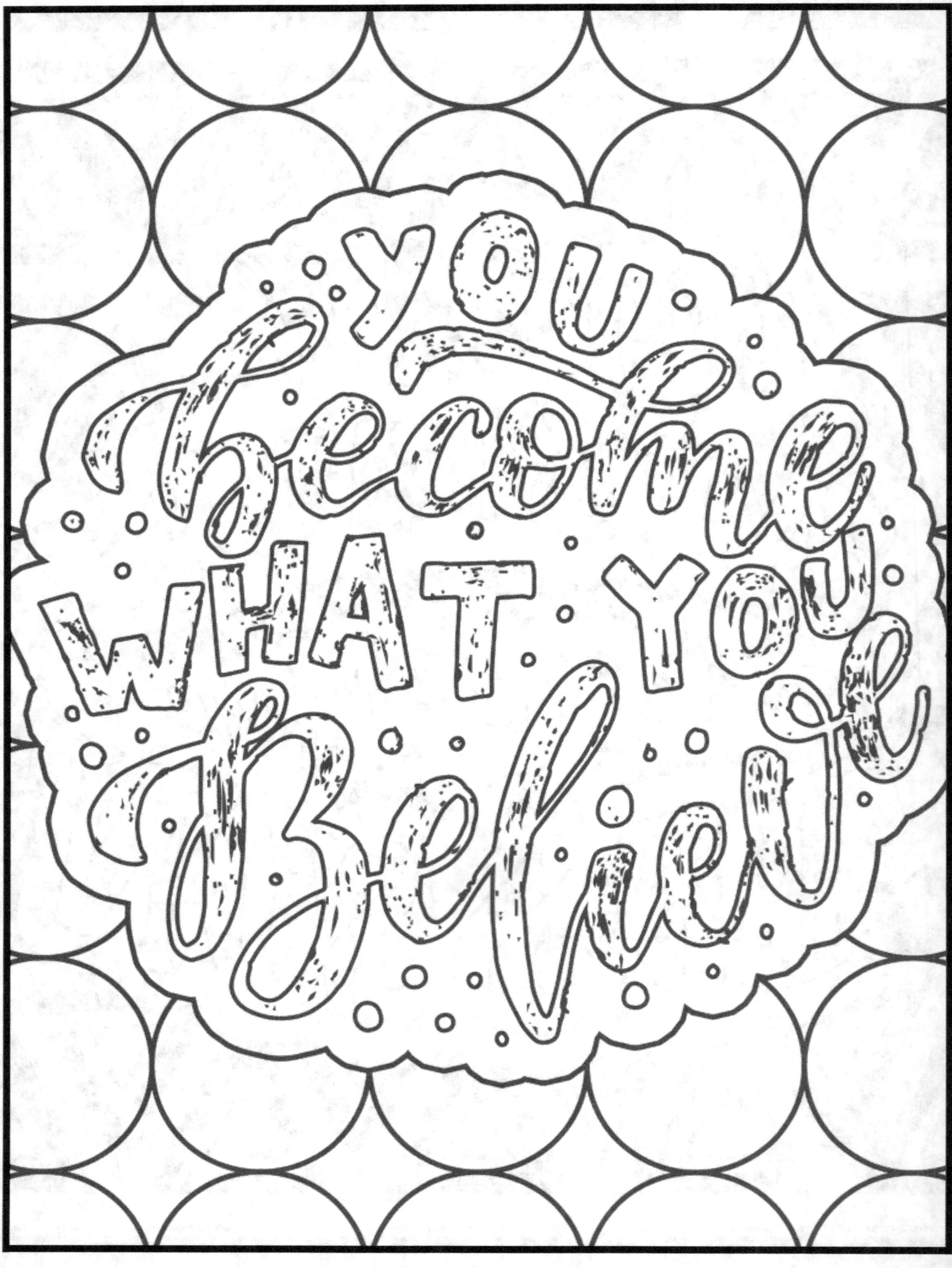
You become what you Believe

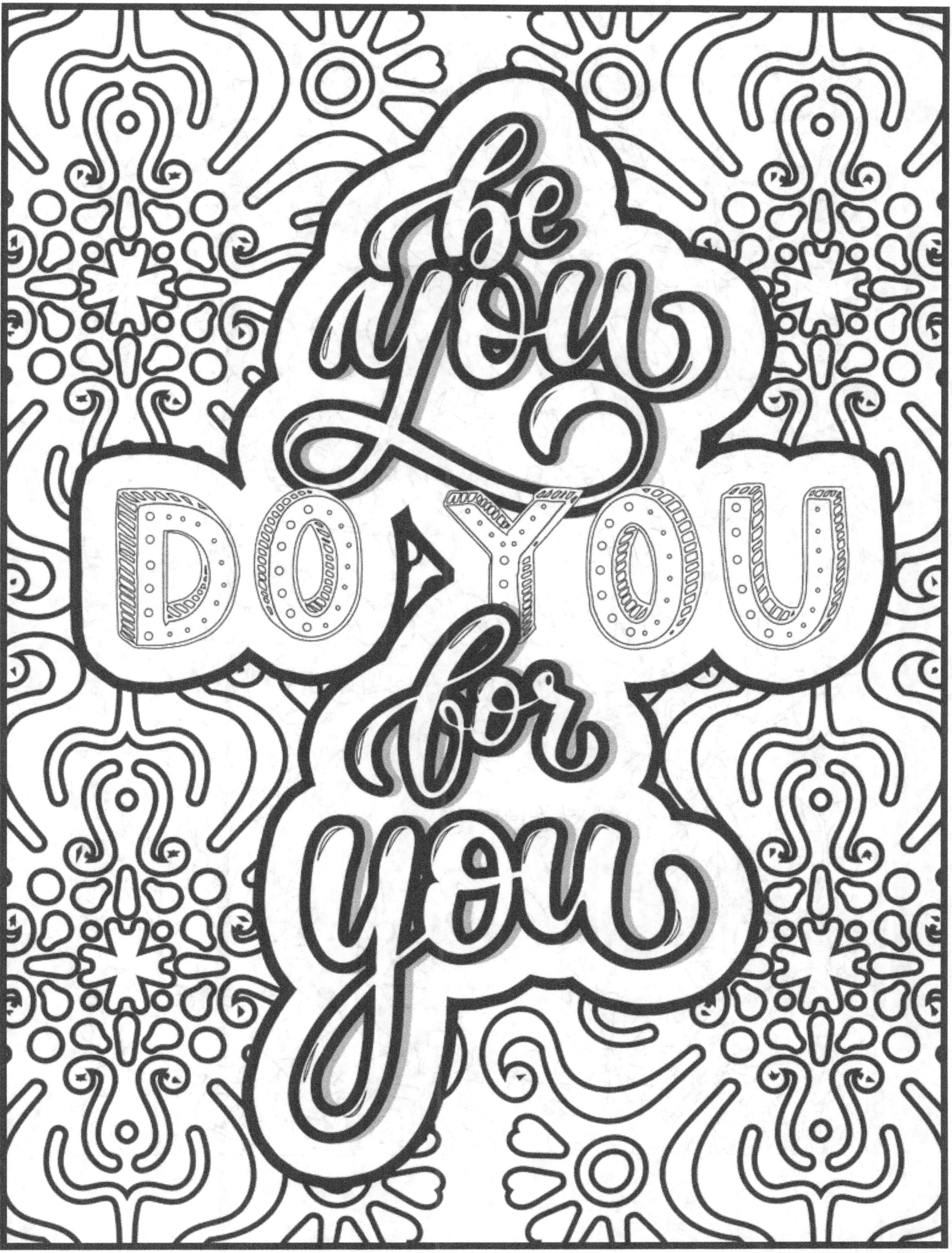
be you
DO YOU
for
you

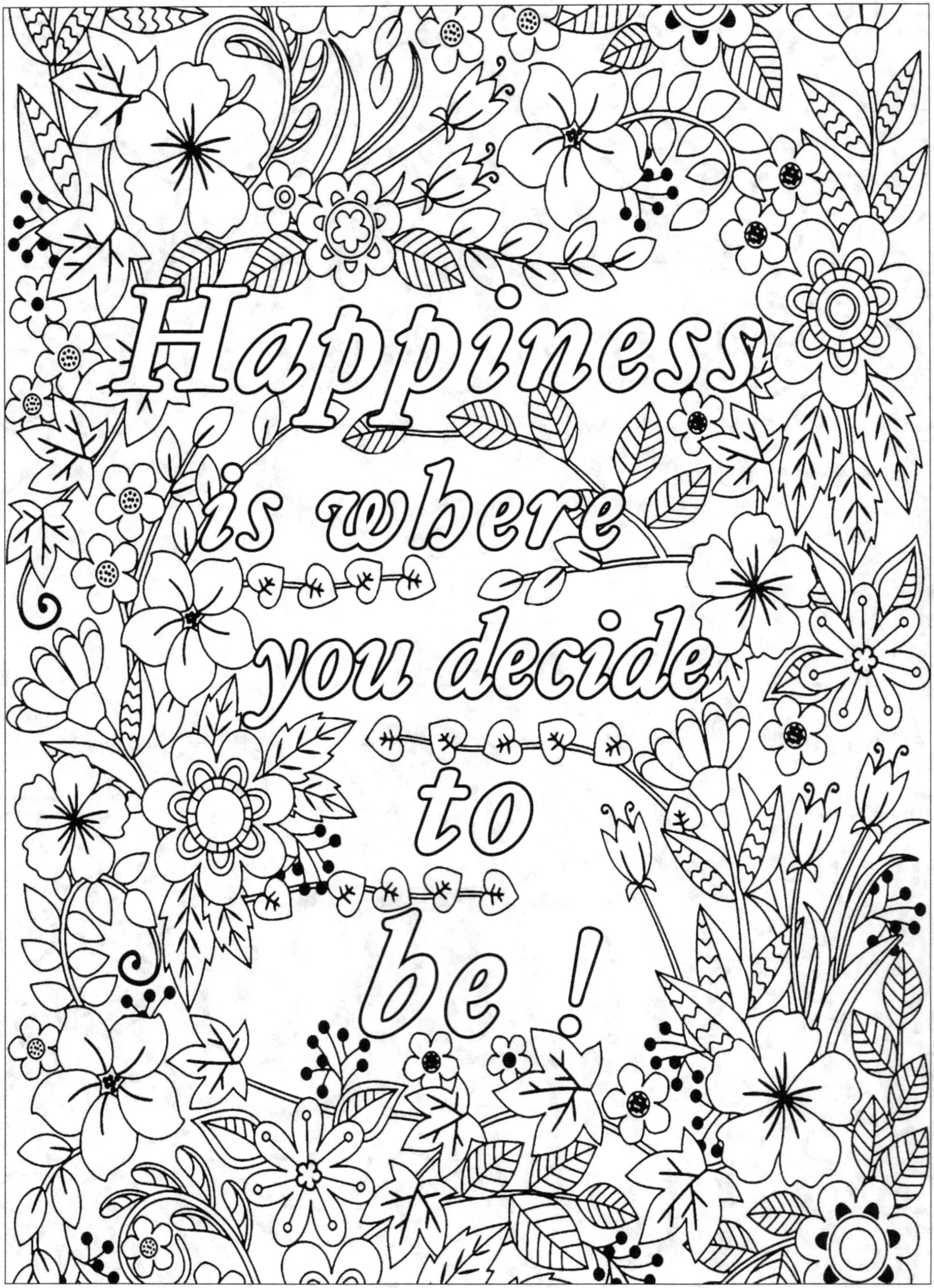
Happiness
is where
you decide
to
be !

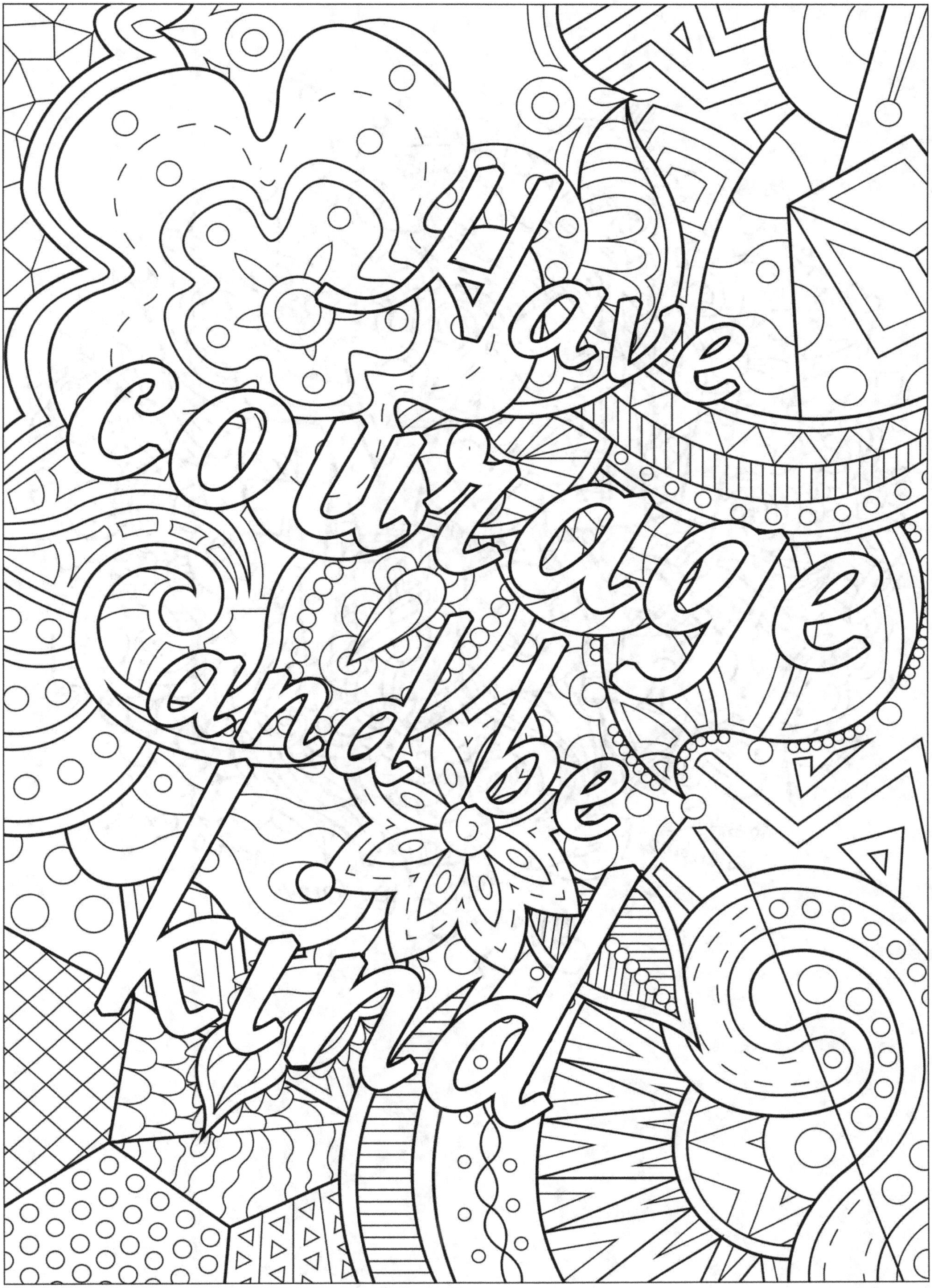
Have
courage
and be
kind

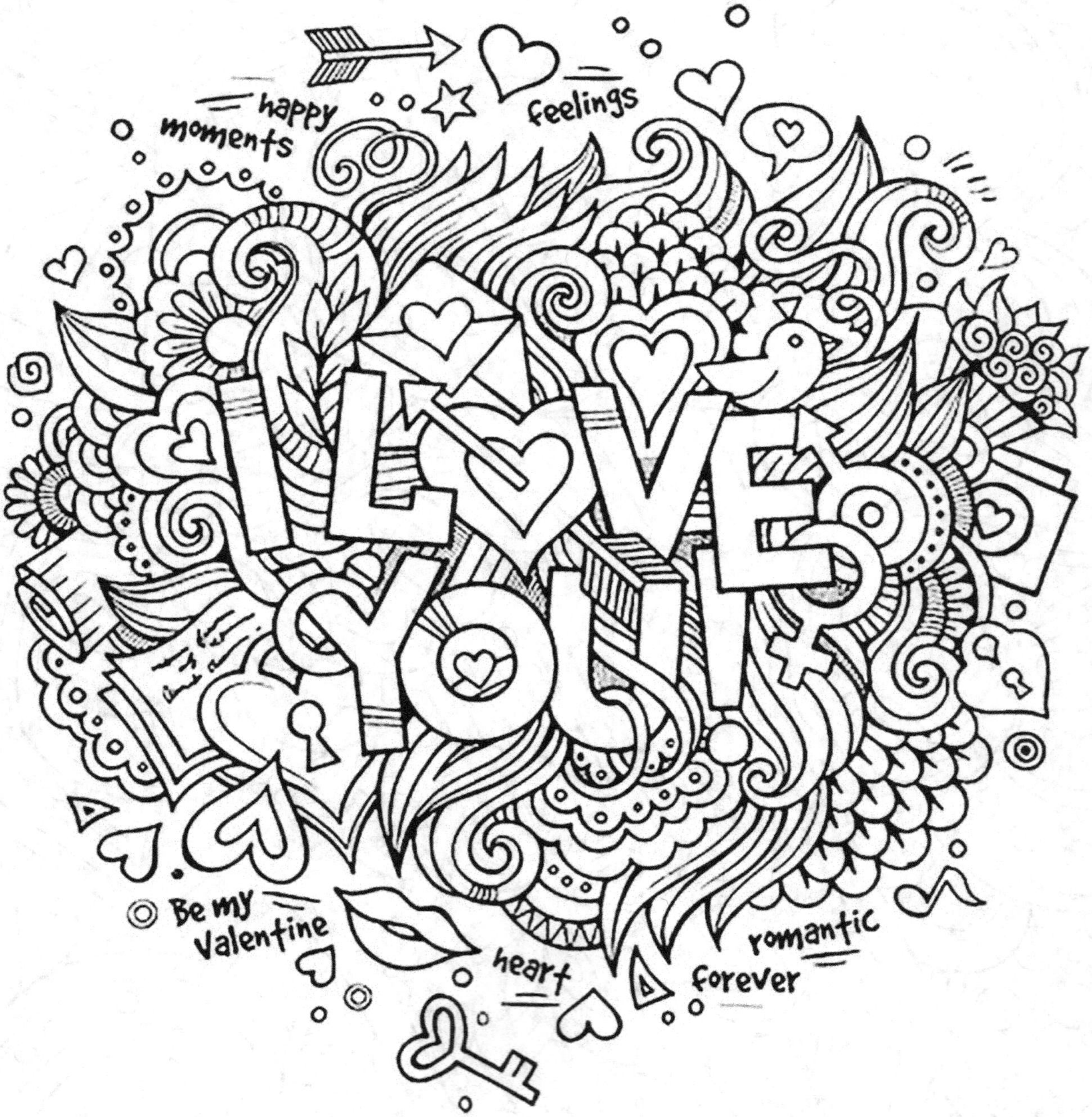
happy moments
feelings
I LOVE YOU!
Be my Valentine
heart
romantic
forever

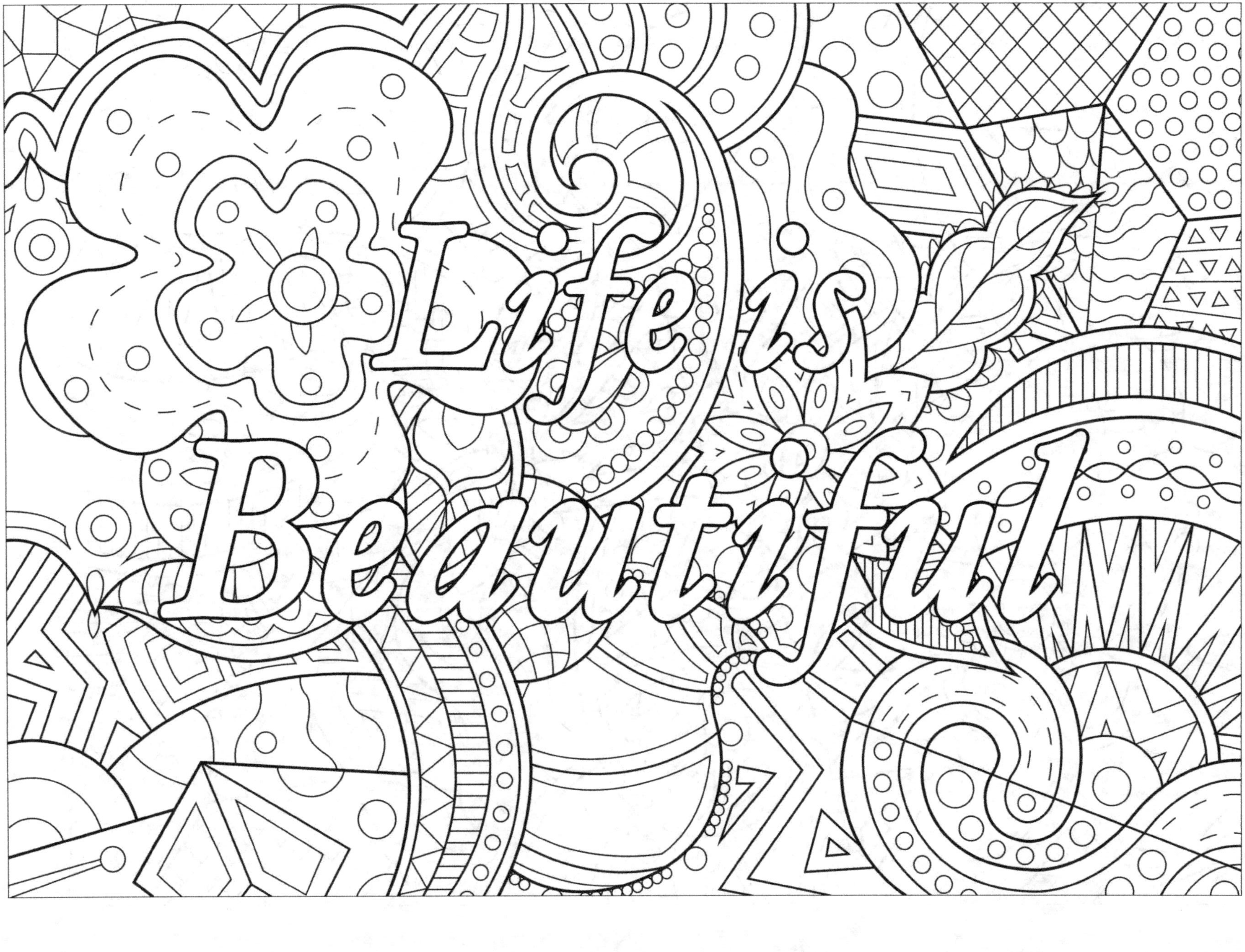
Life is
Beautiful

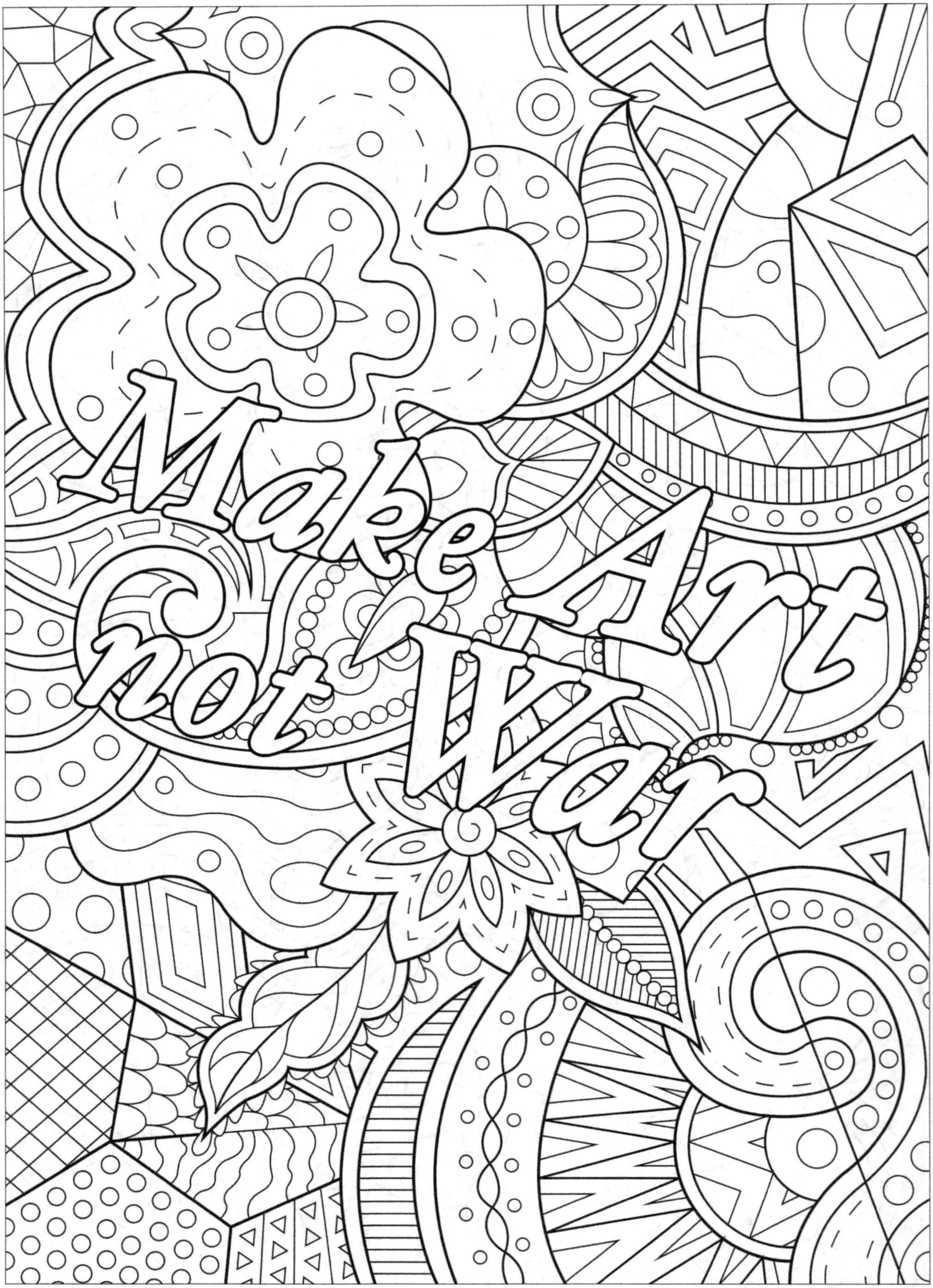
Make Art
not War

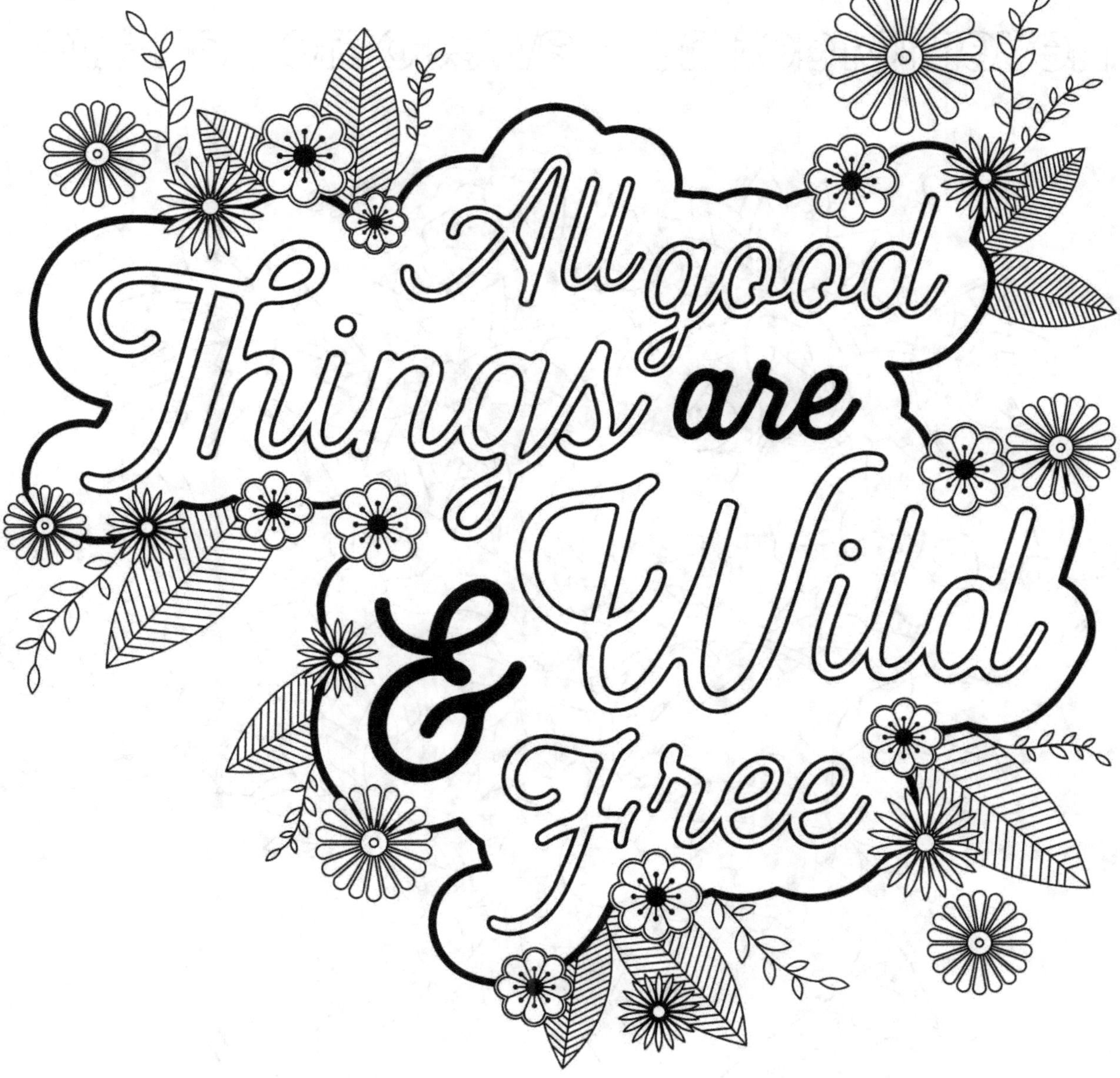
All good
Things are
& Wild
Free

Good Morning

never forget how awesome you are

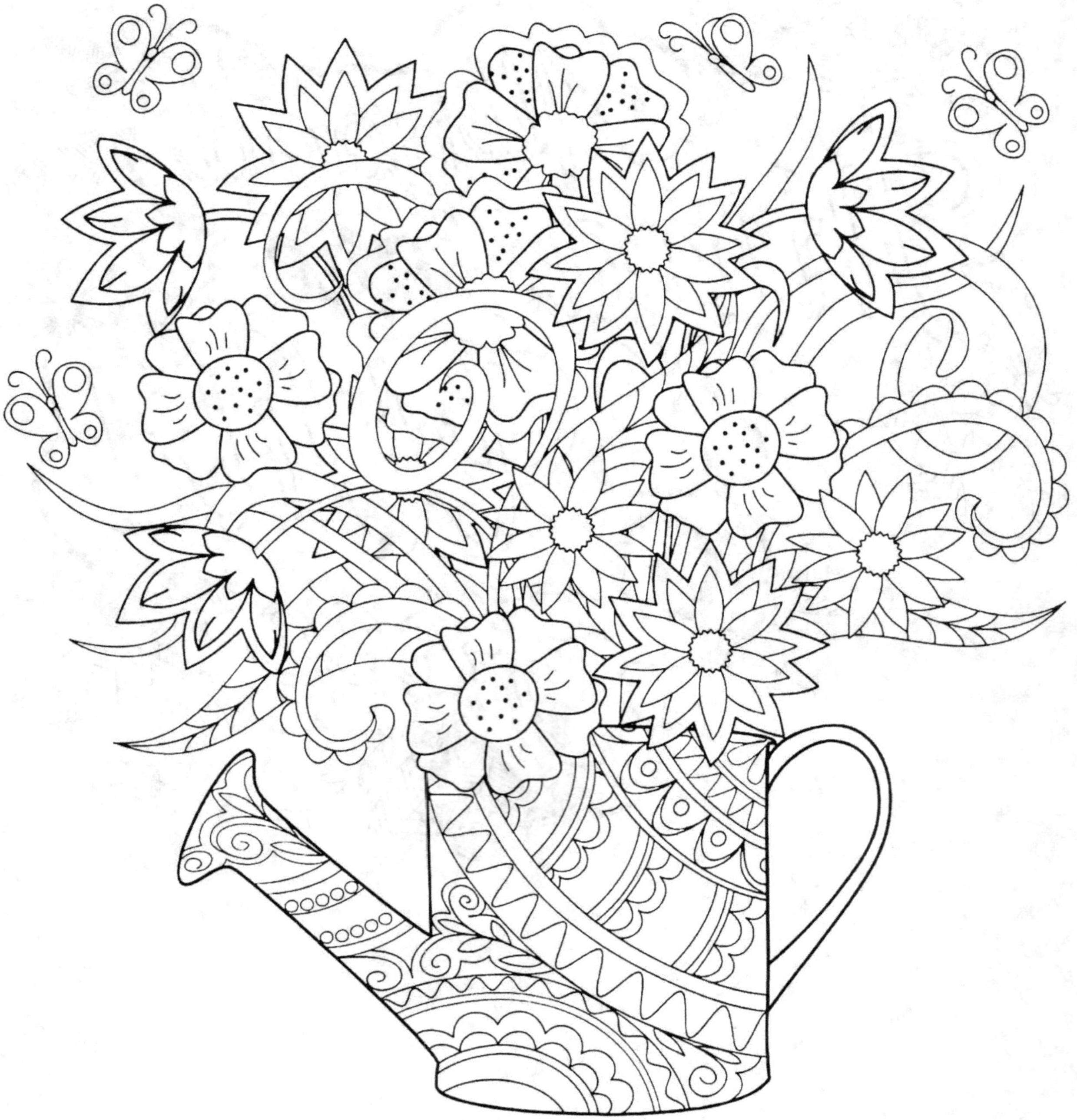

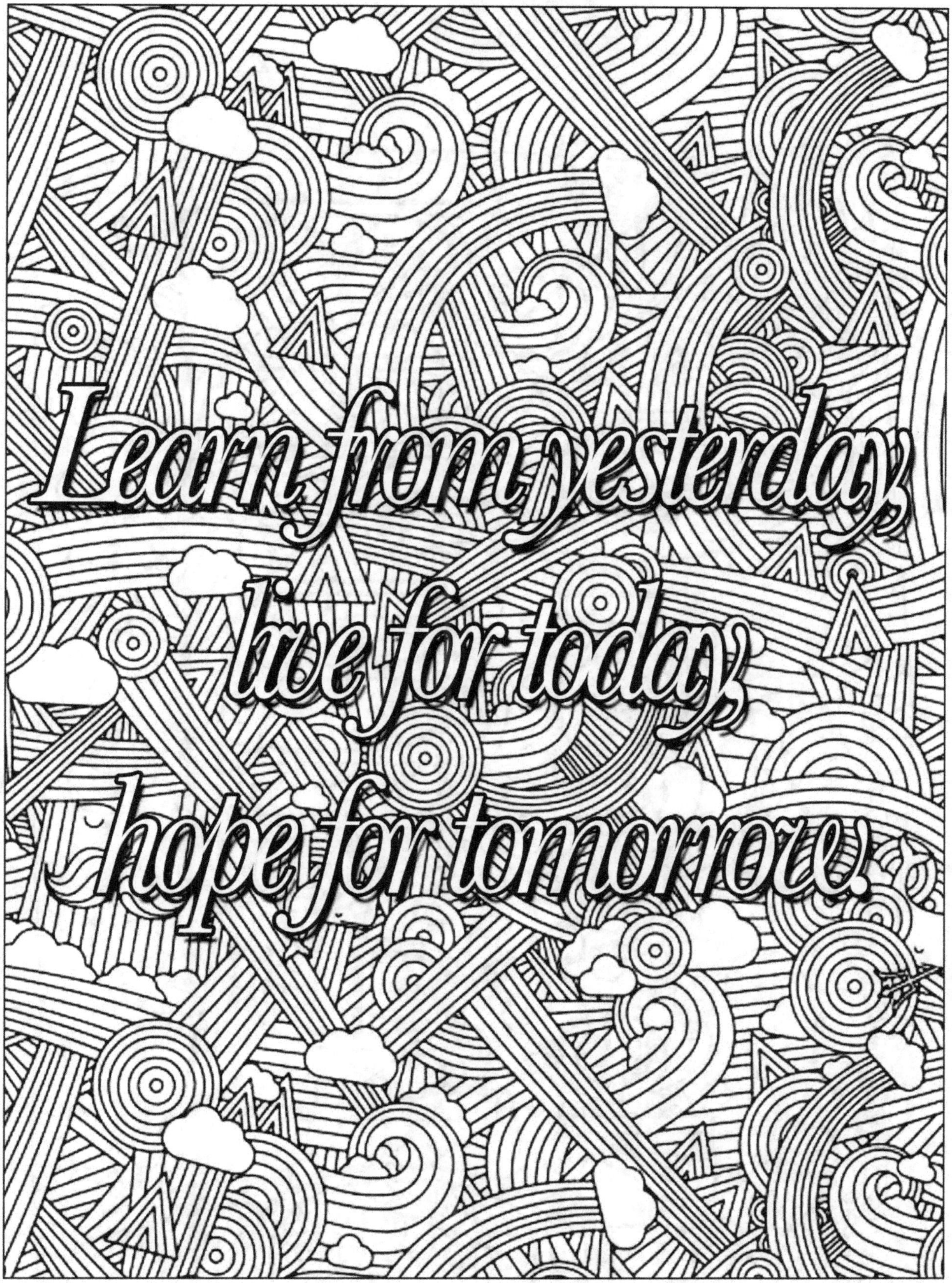
Learn from yesterday,
live for today,
hope for tomorrow.

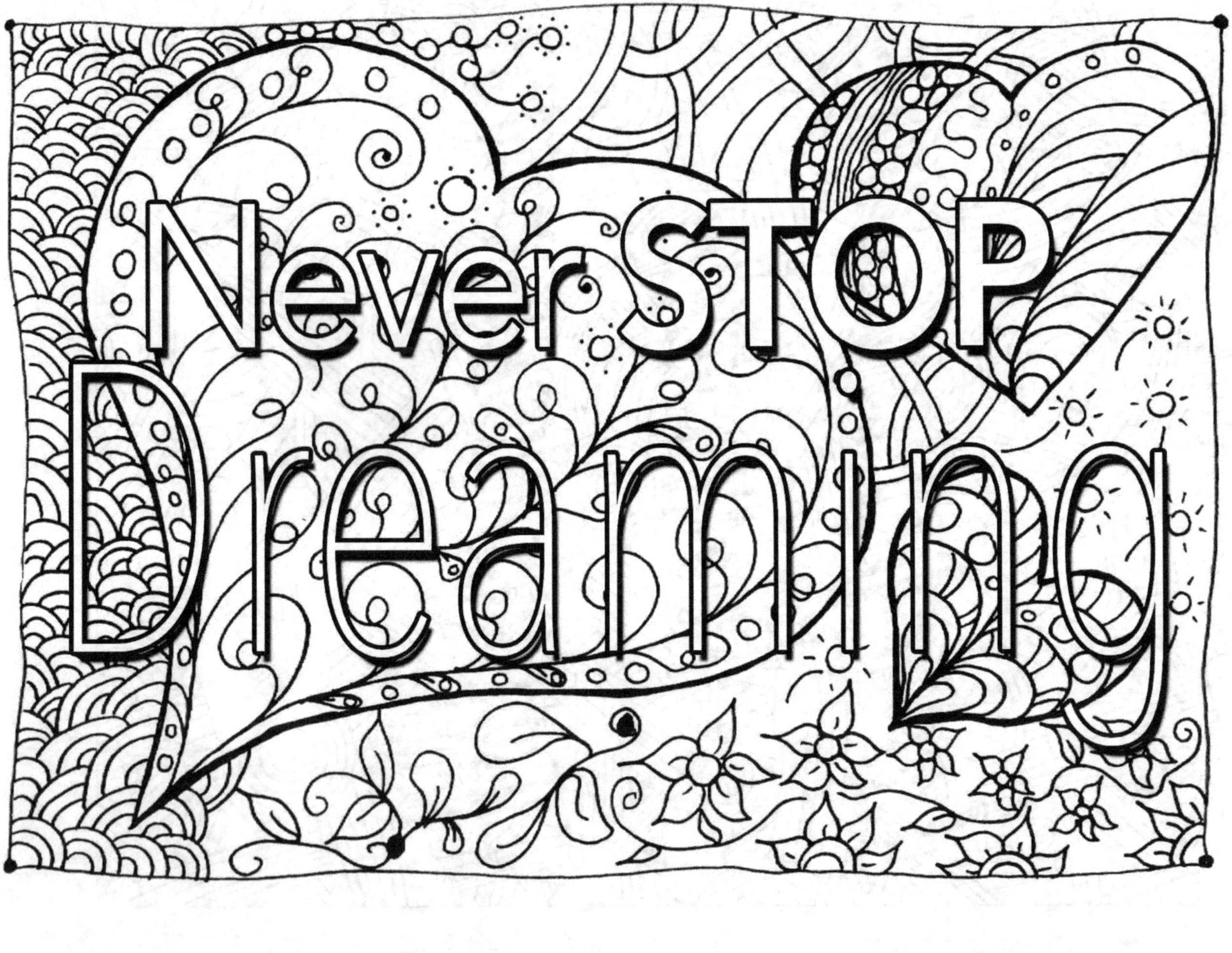
Never STOP
Dreaming

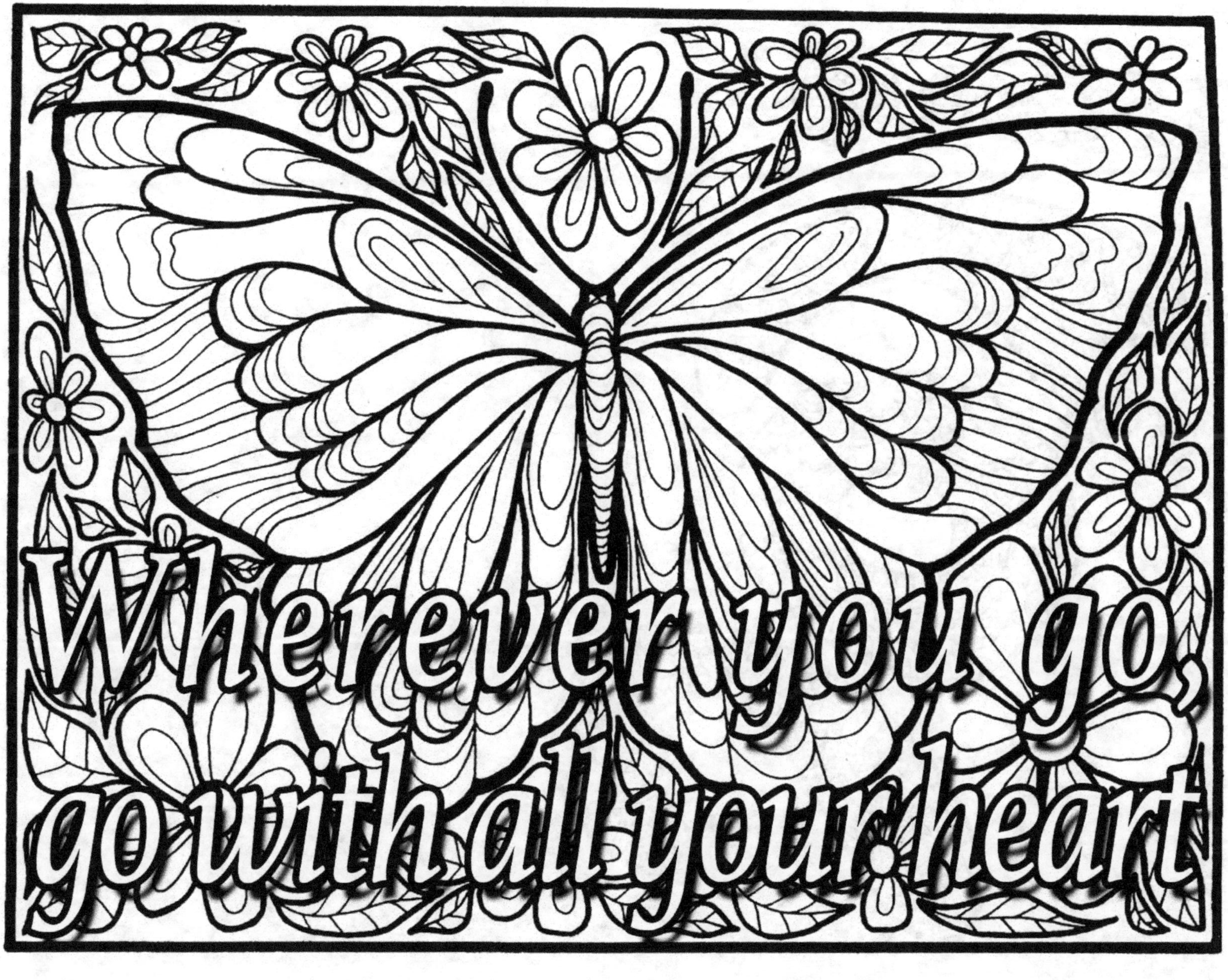
Wherever you go,
go with all your heart

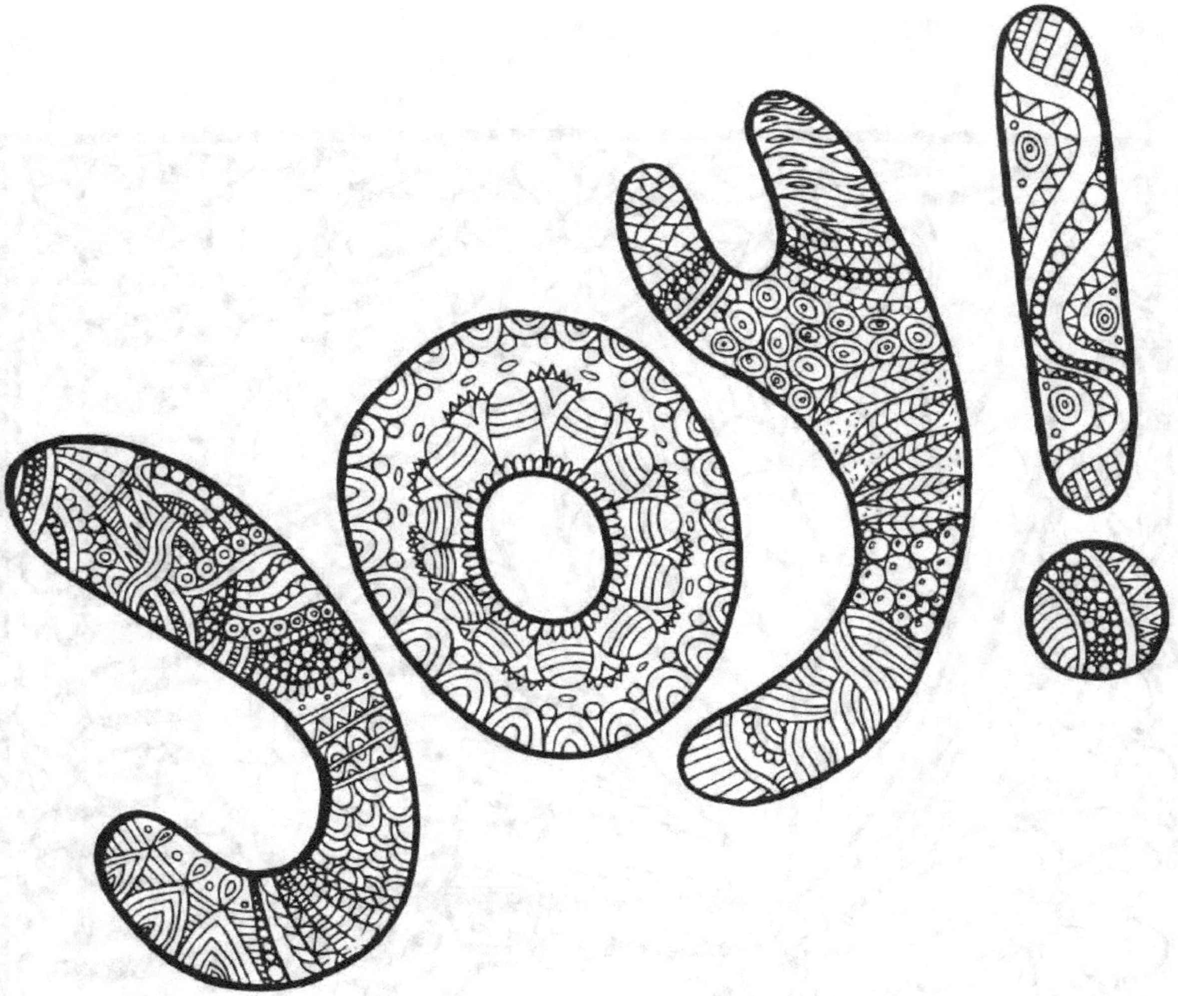
JOY!

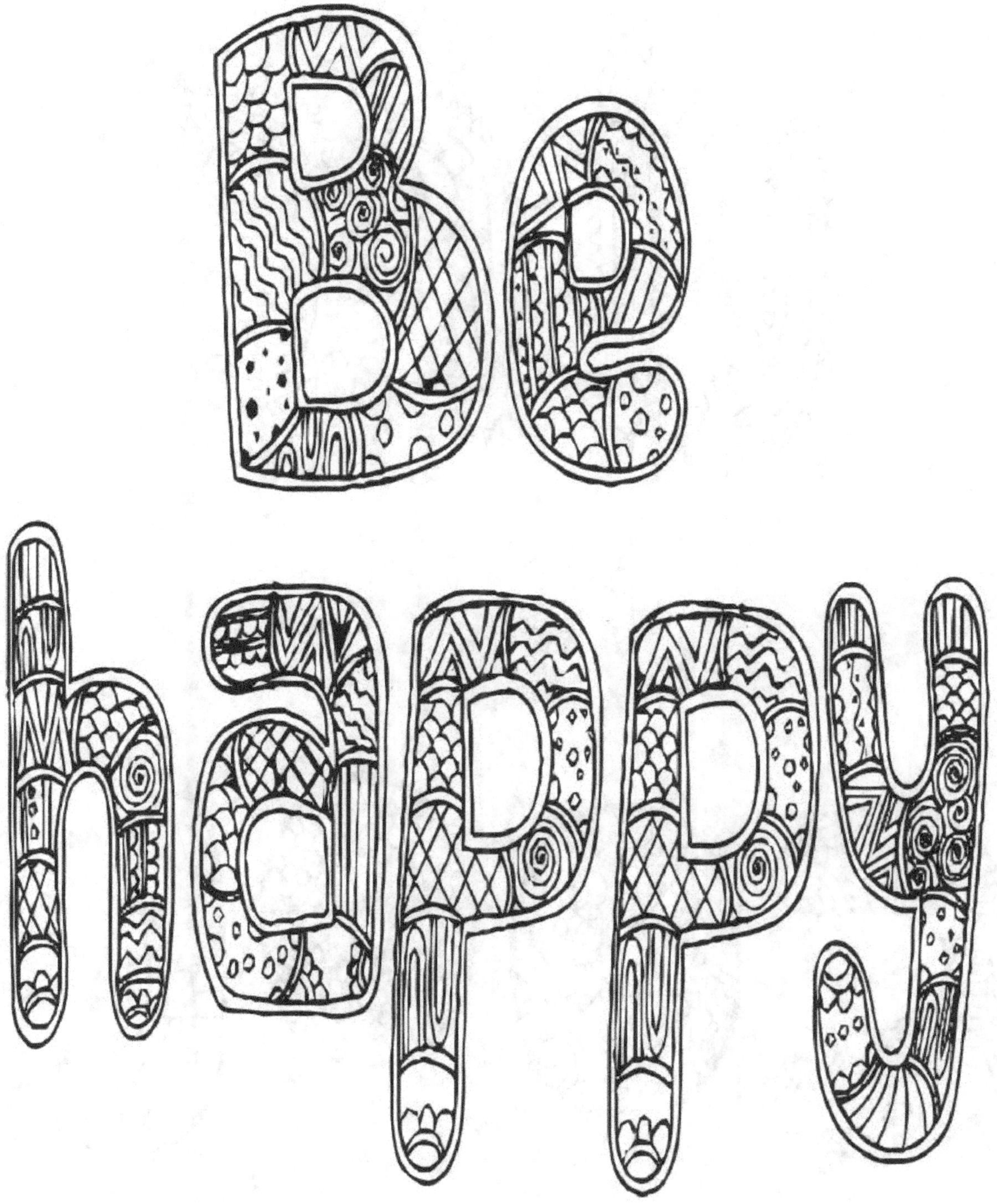
Be
happy

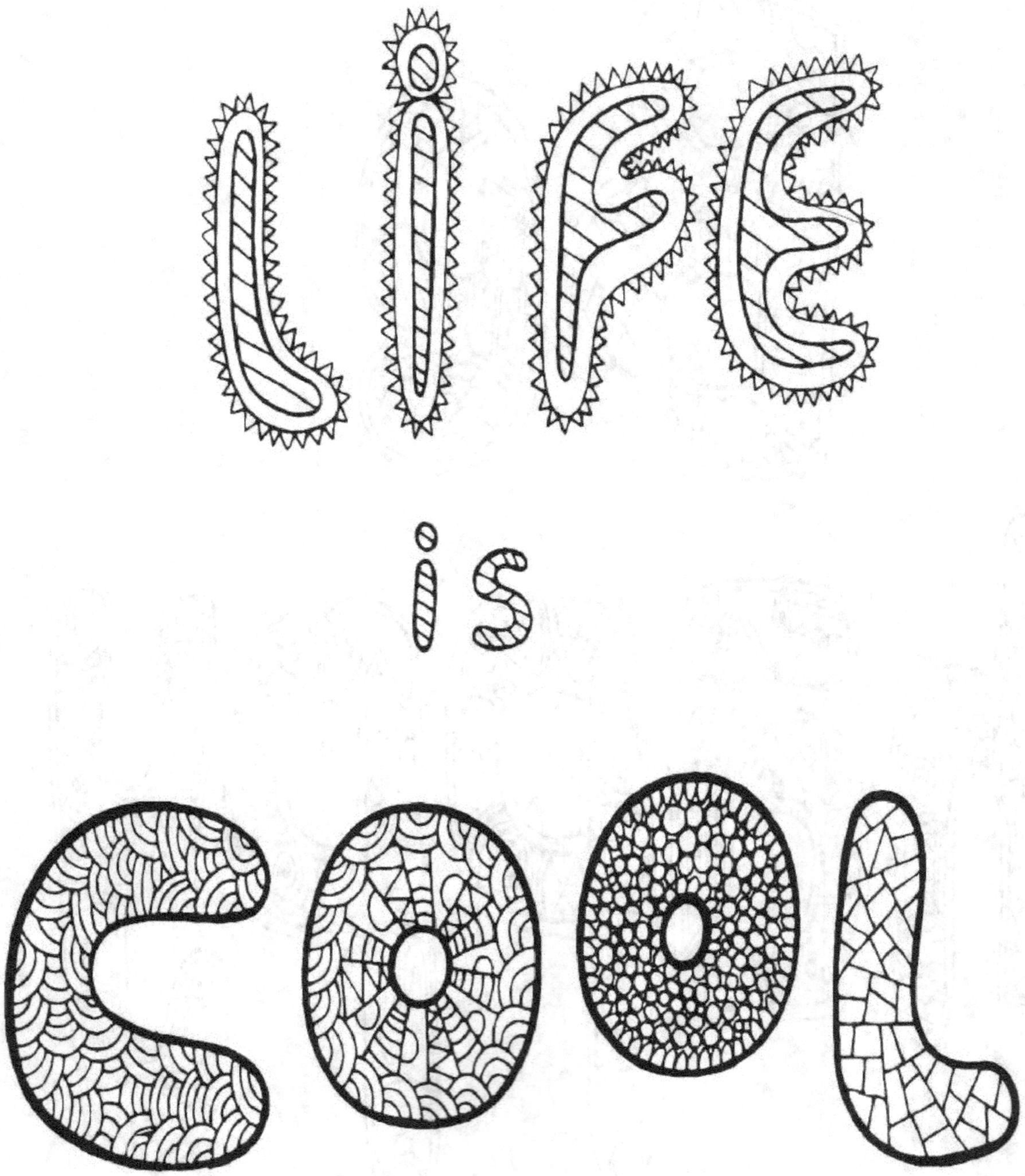
LIFE
is
COOL

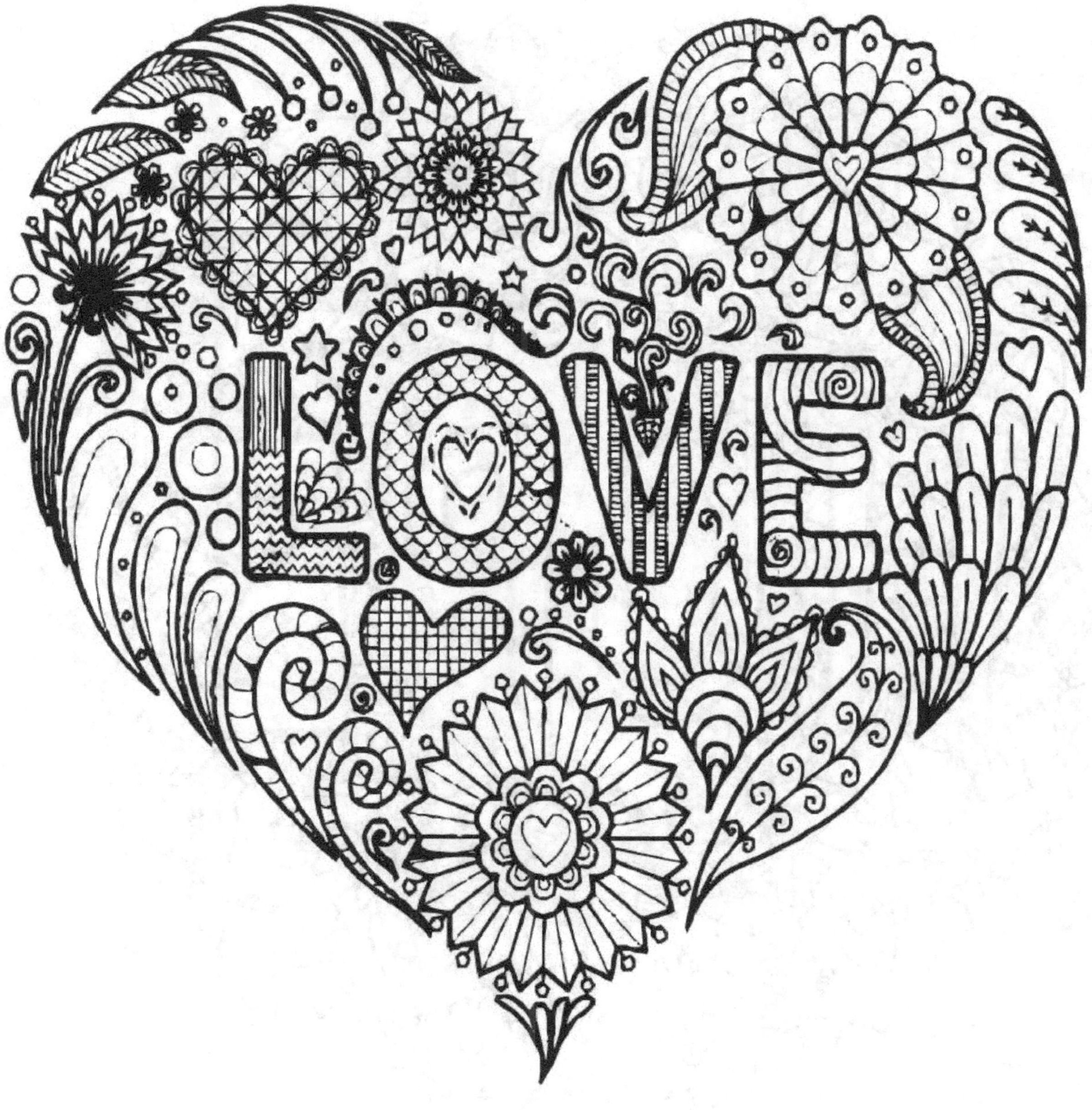
LOVE

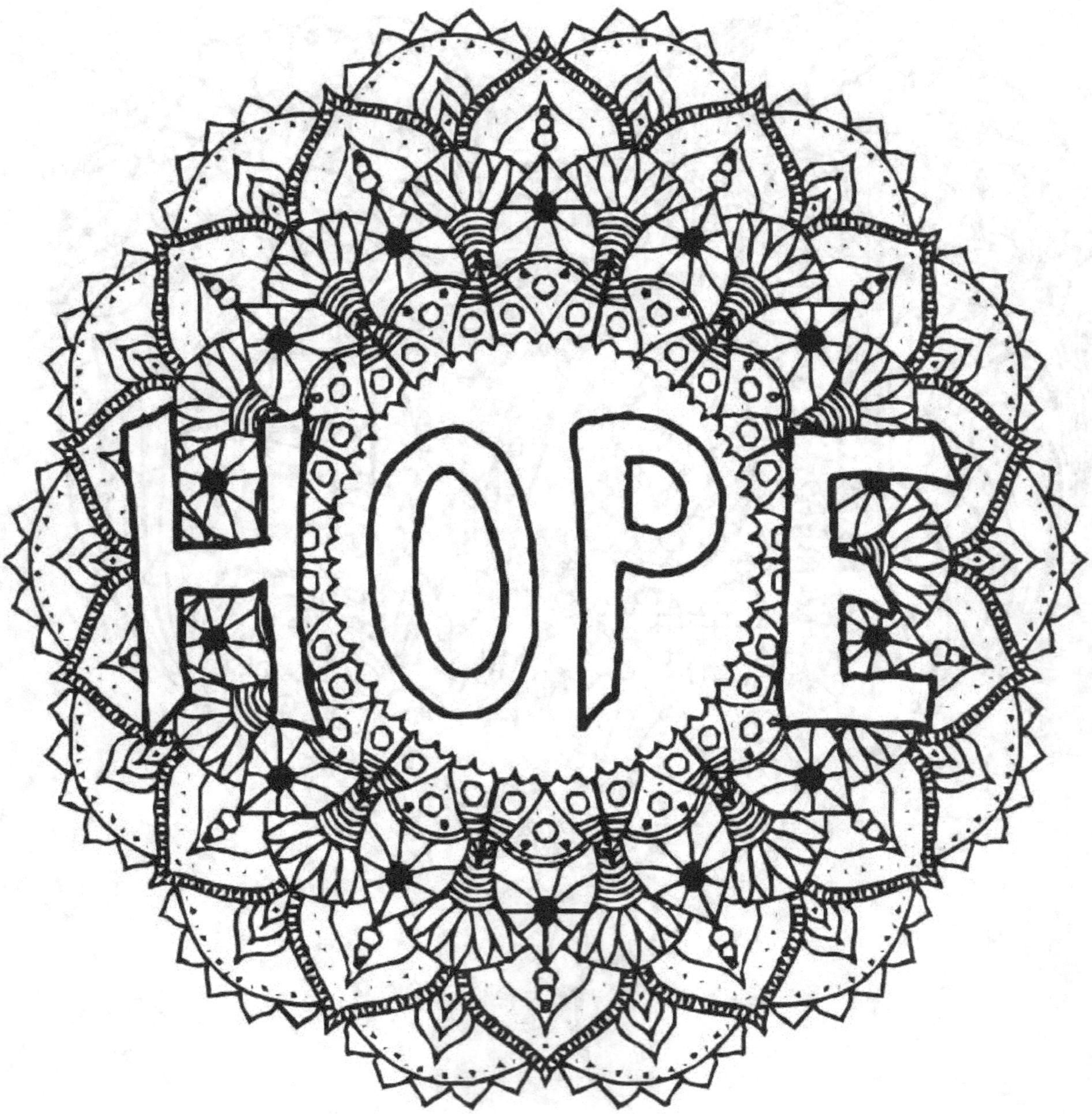
HOPE

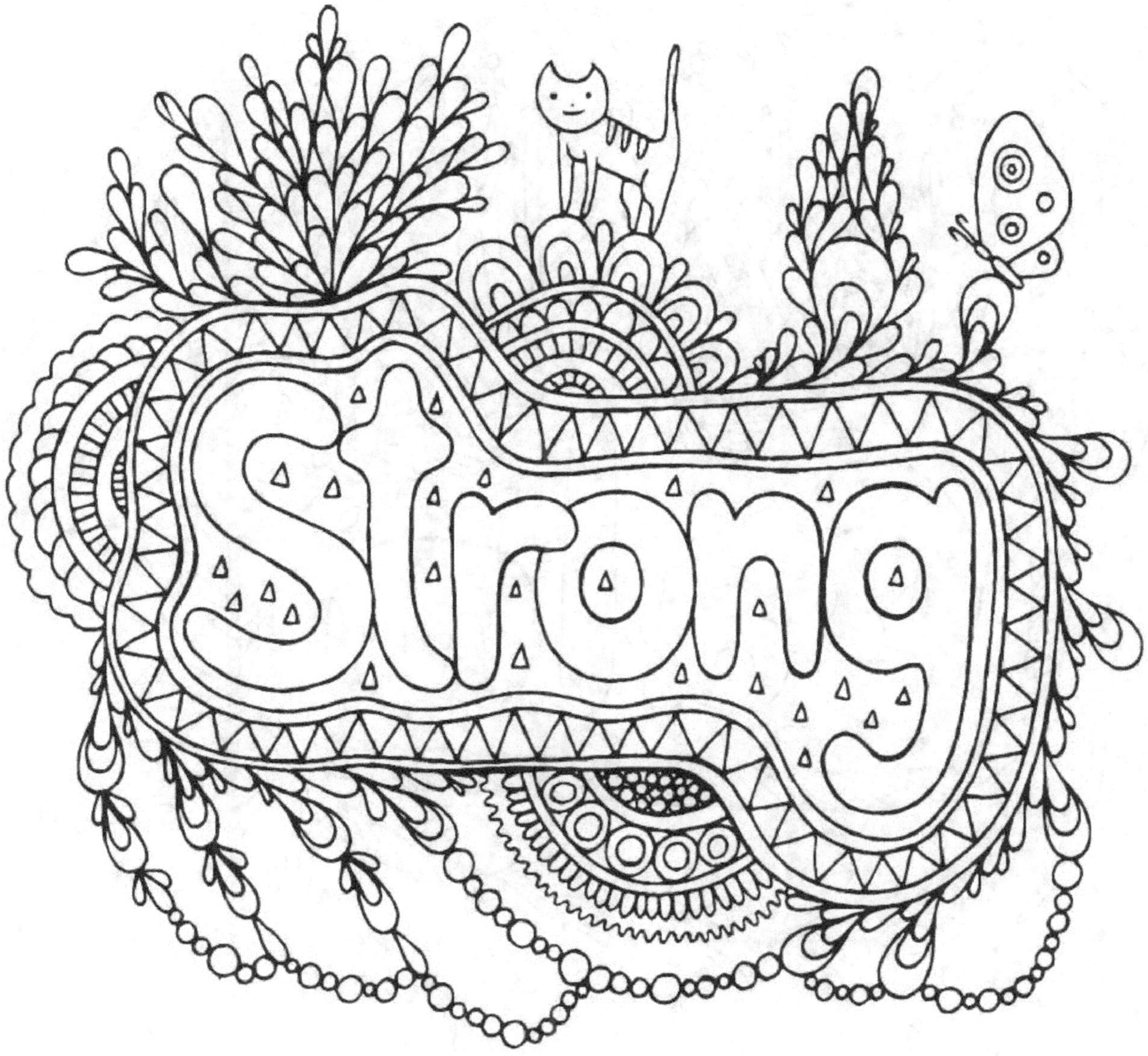
Strong

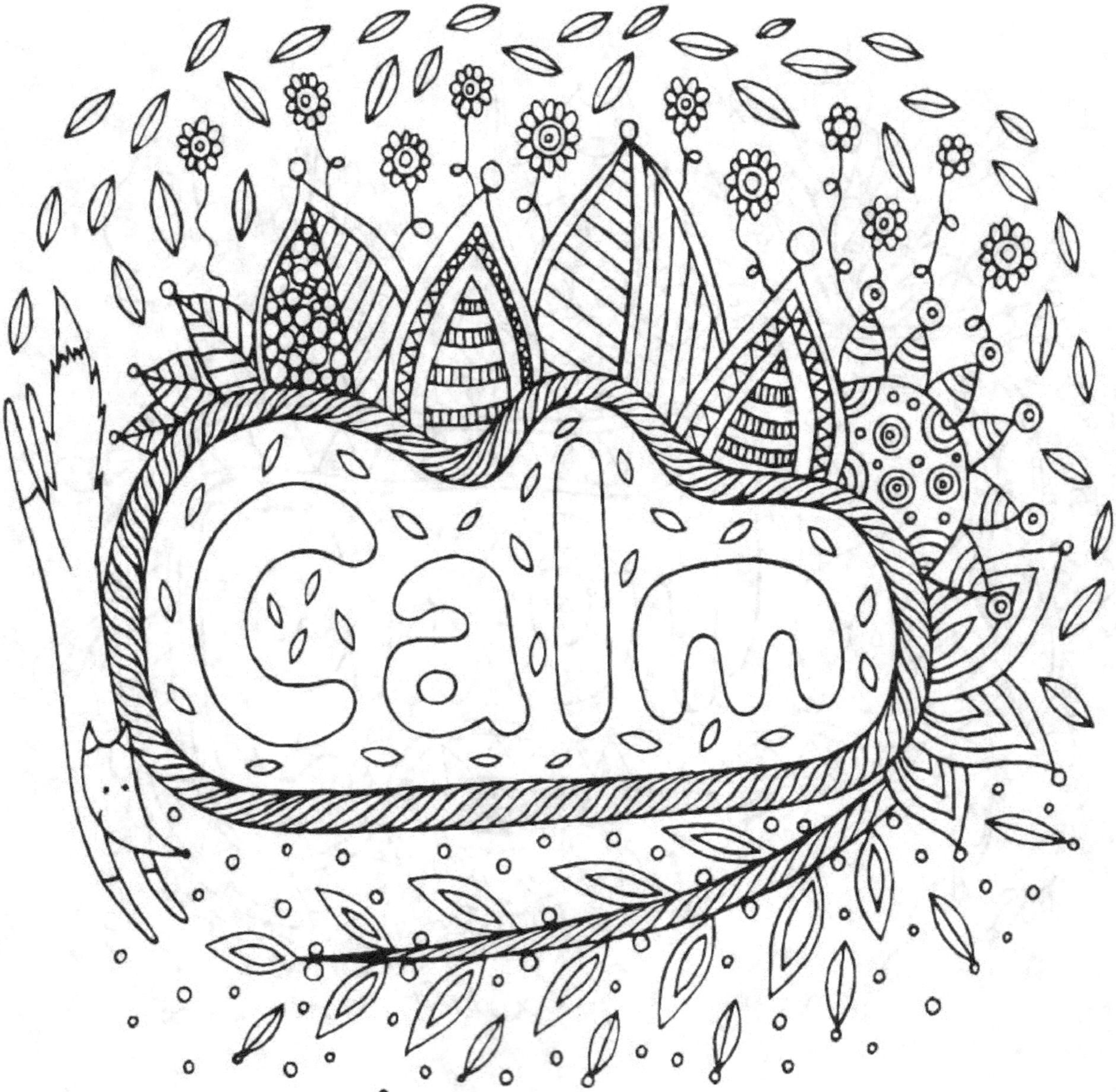
Calm

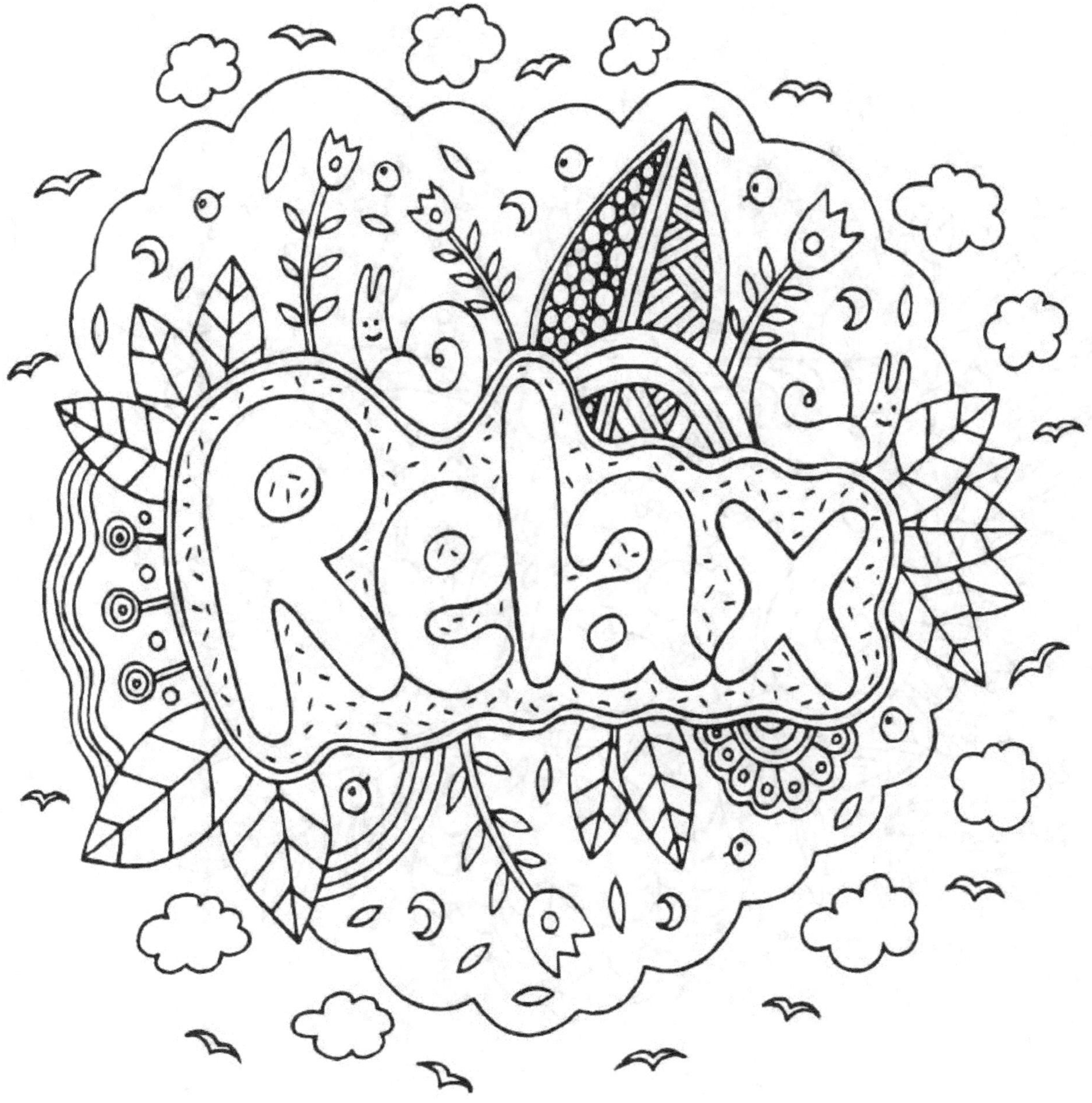
Relax

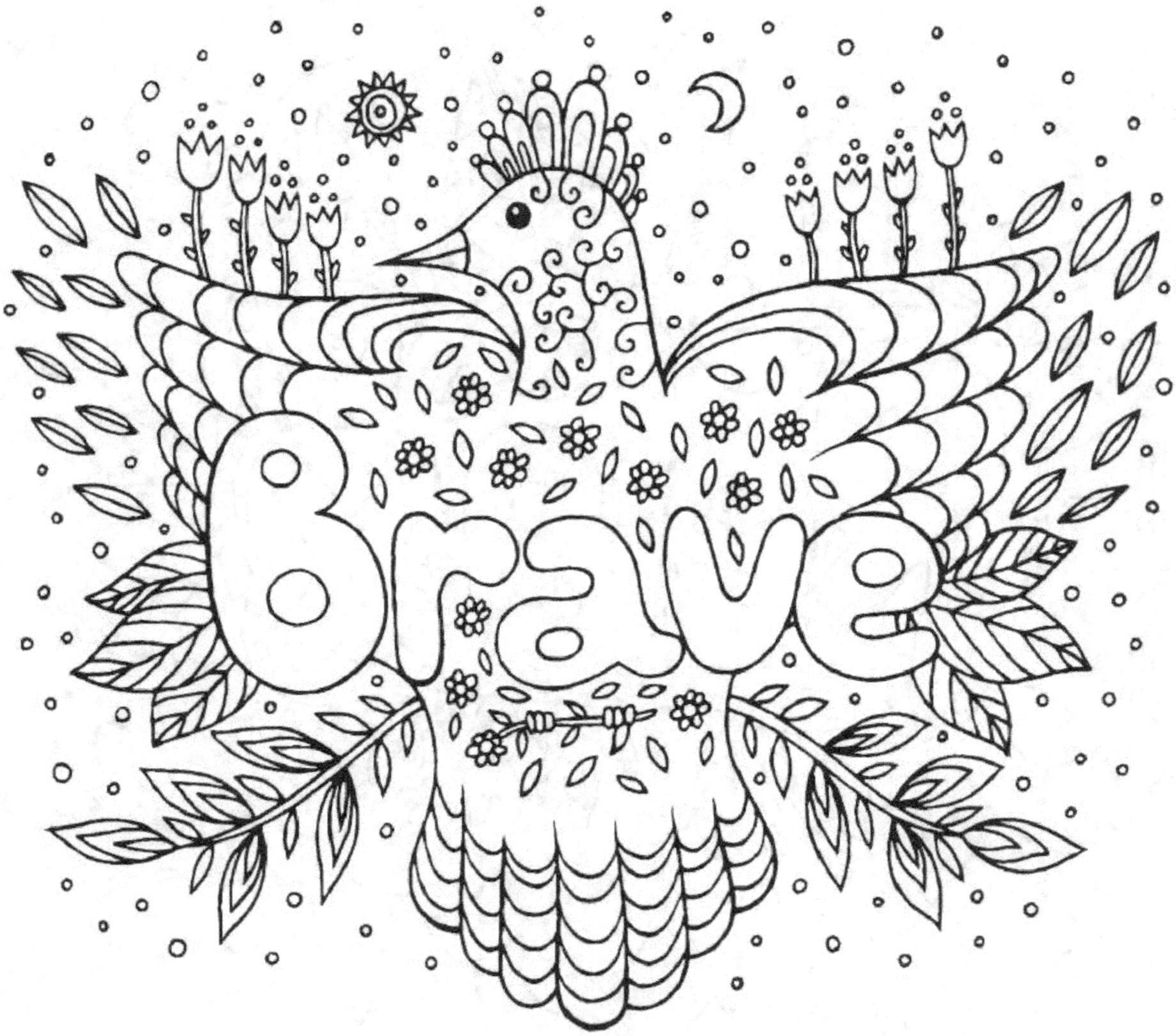
Brave

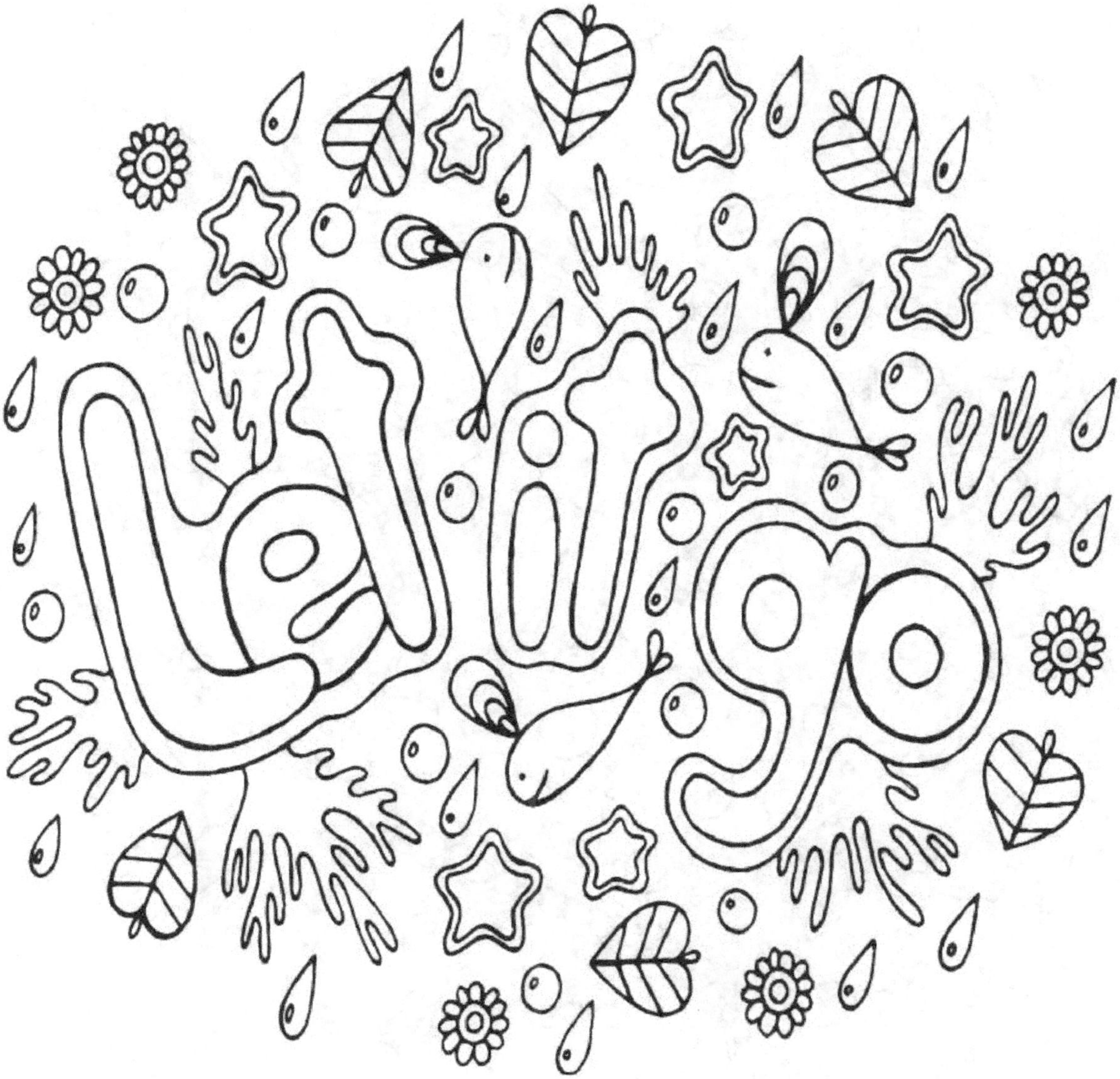
Let it go

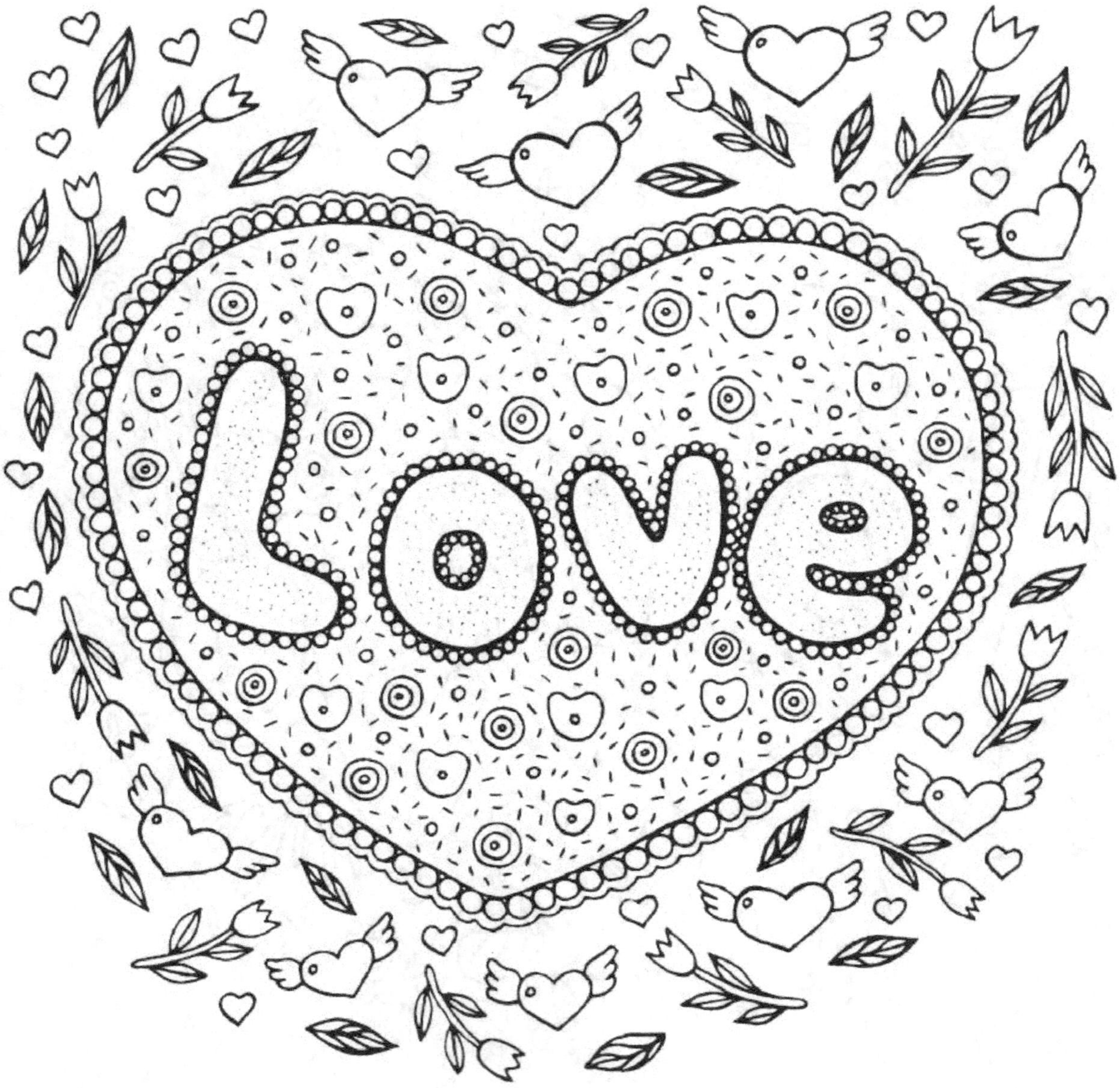
Love

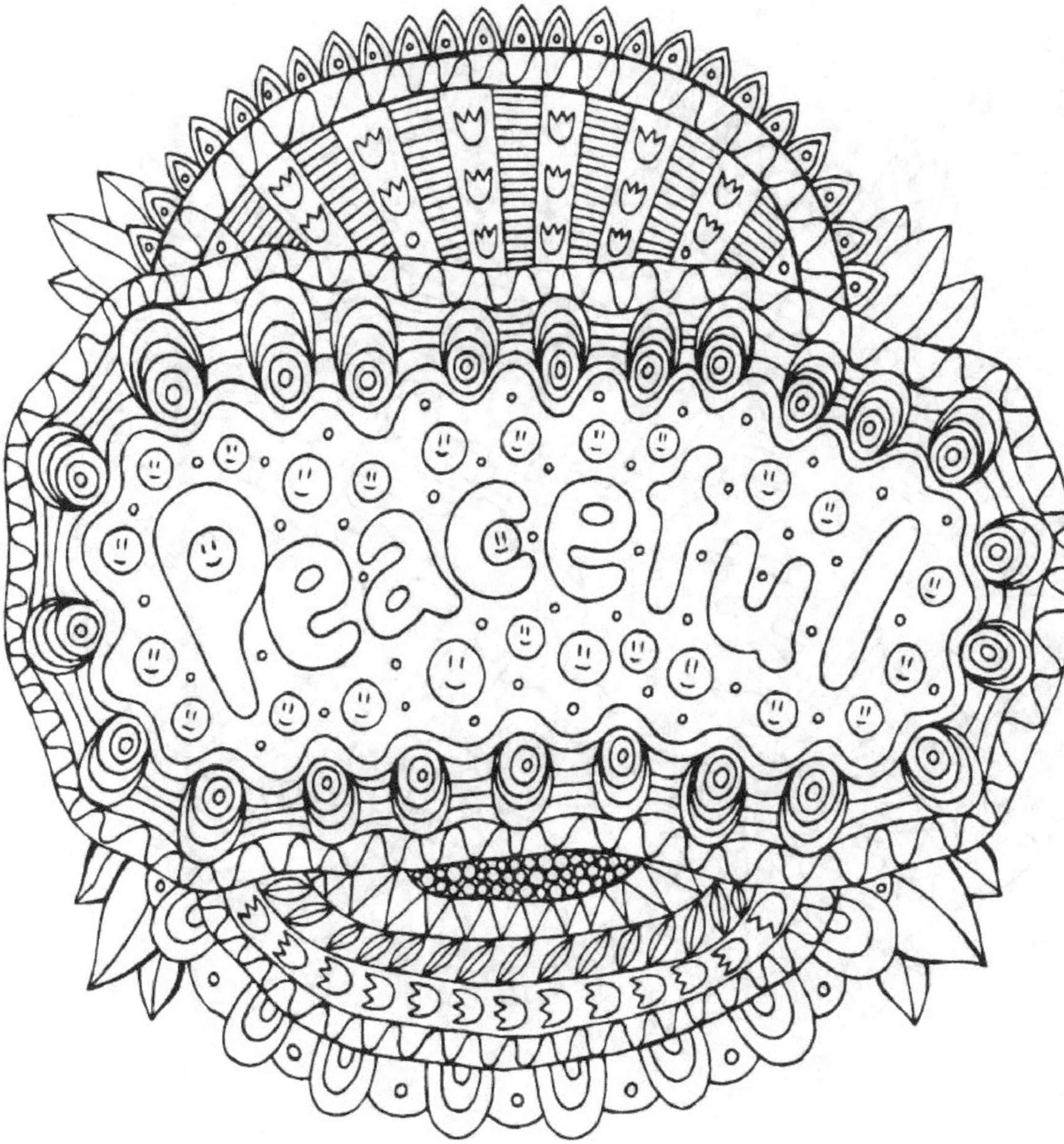
Peaceful

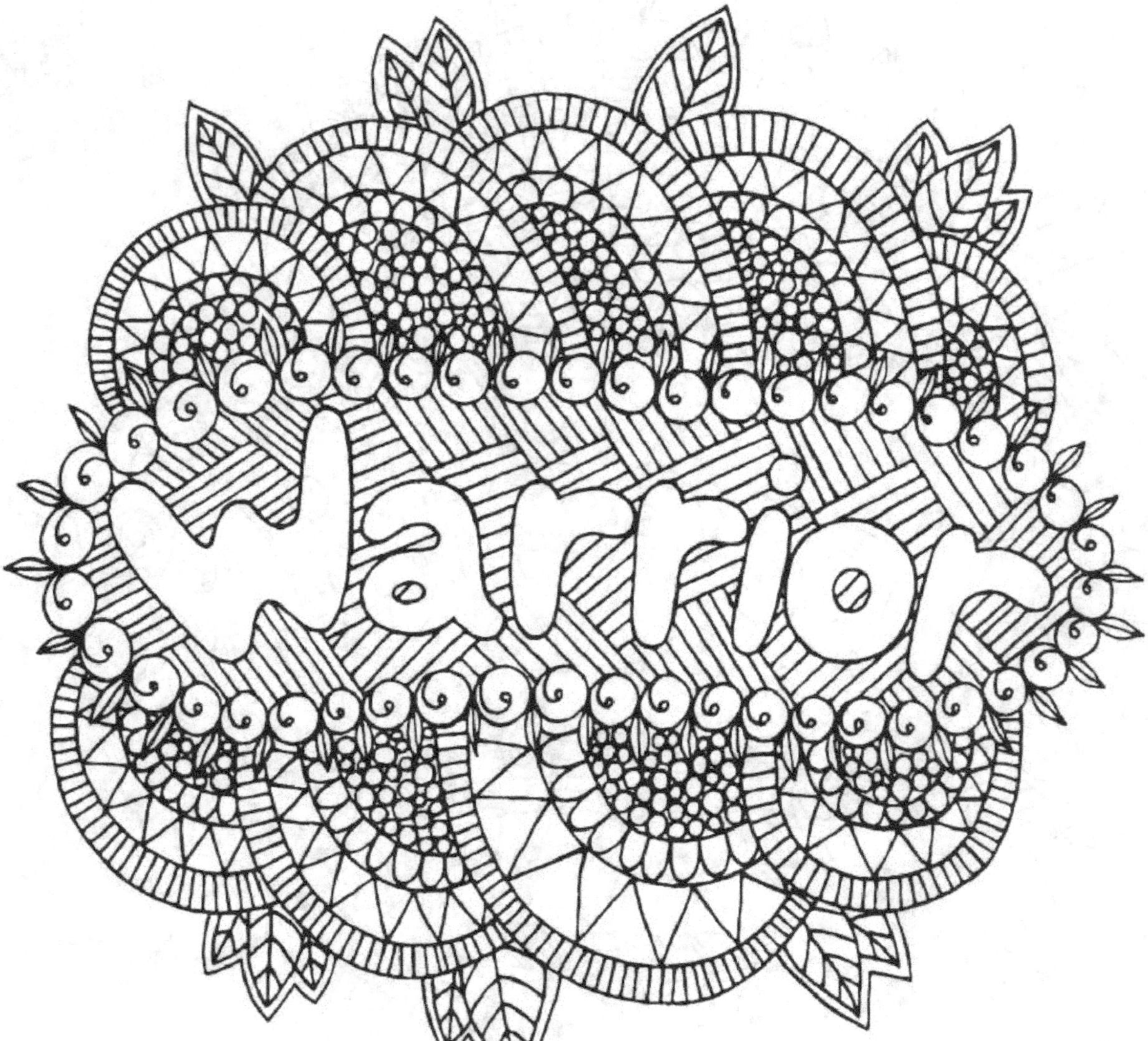
Warrior

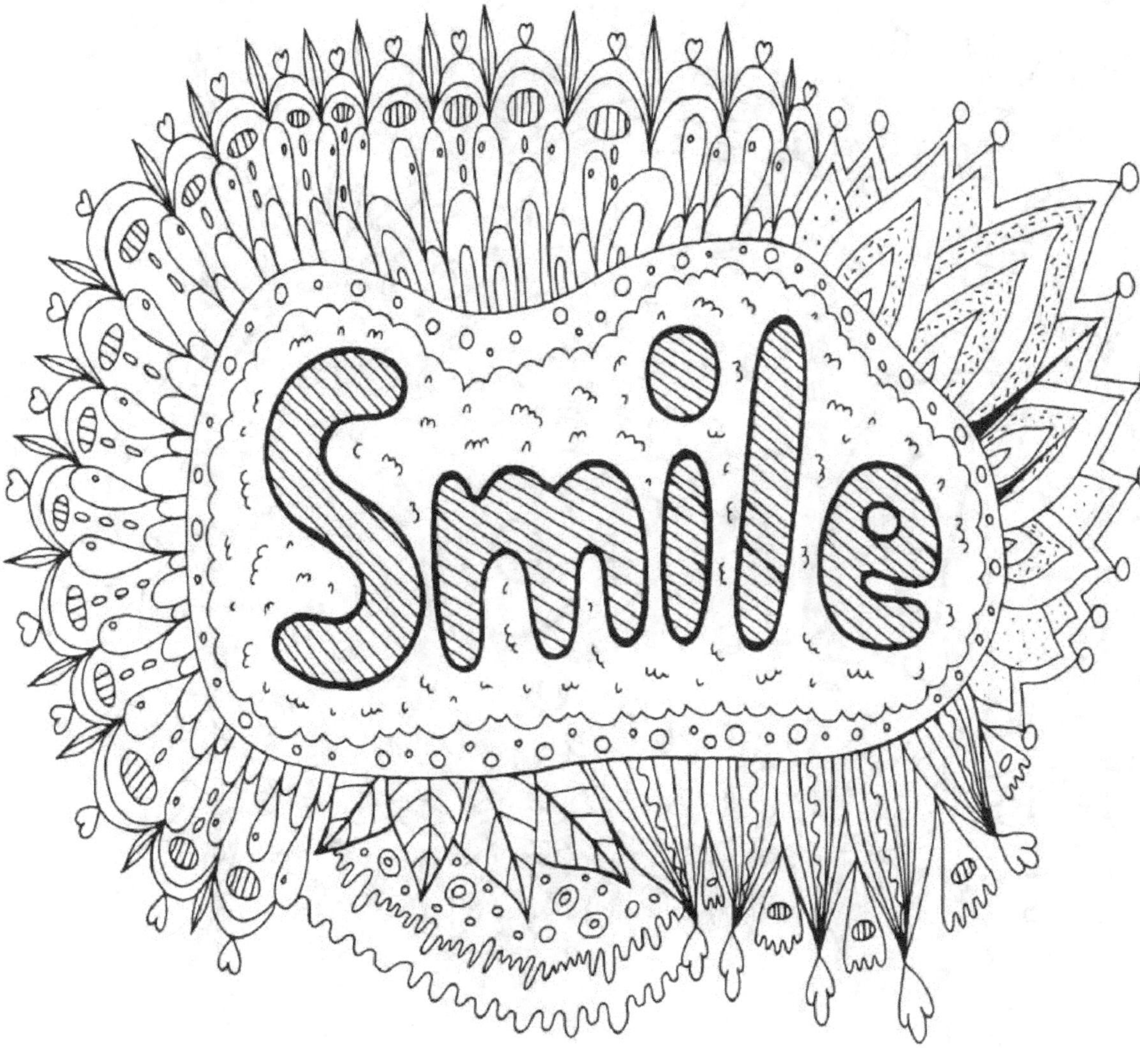
Smile

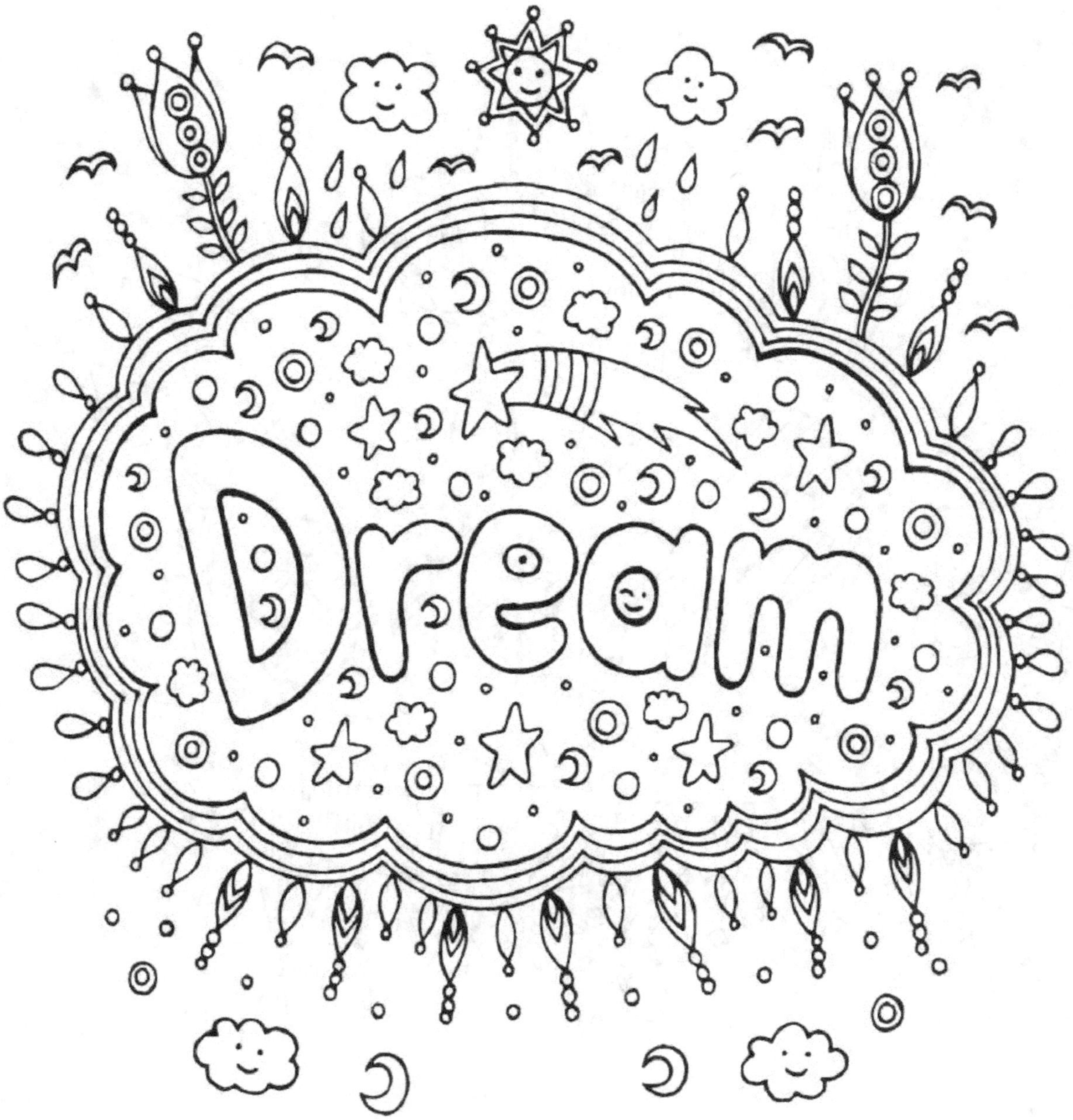
Dream

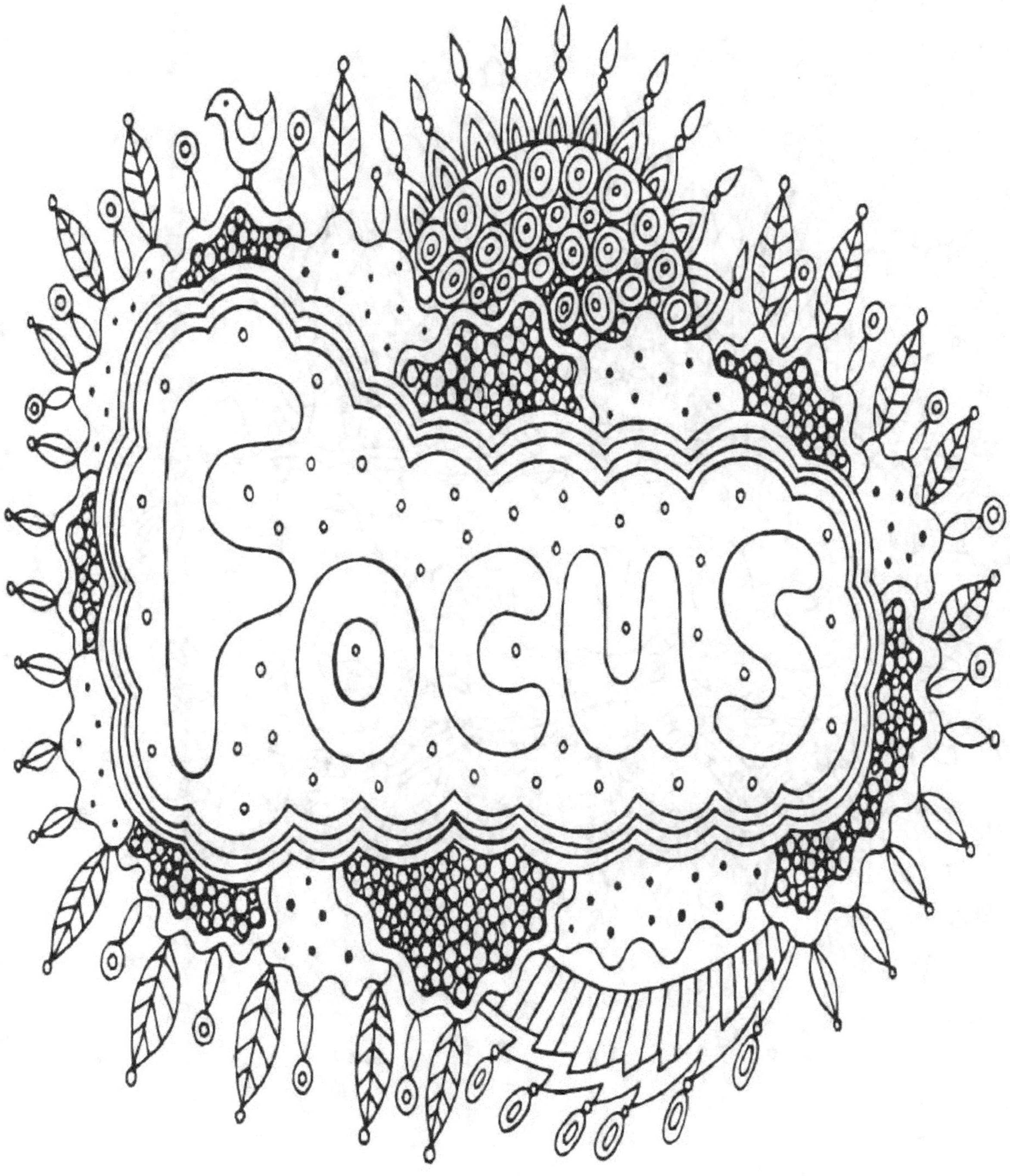
Focus

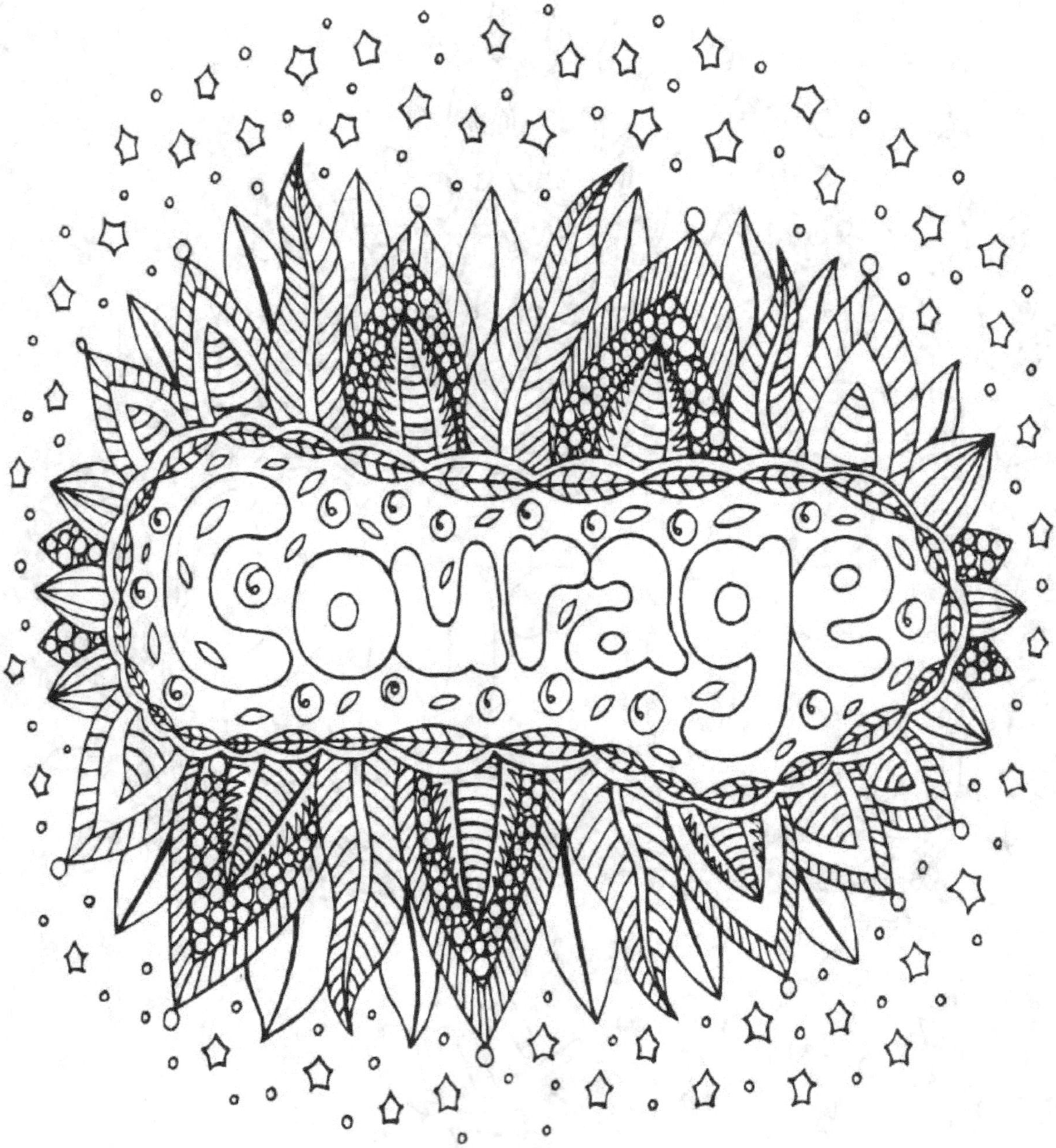
Courage

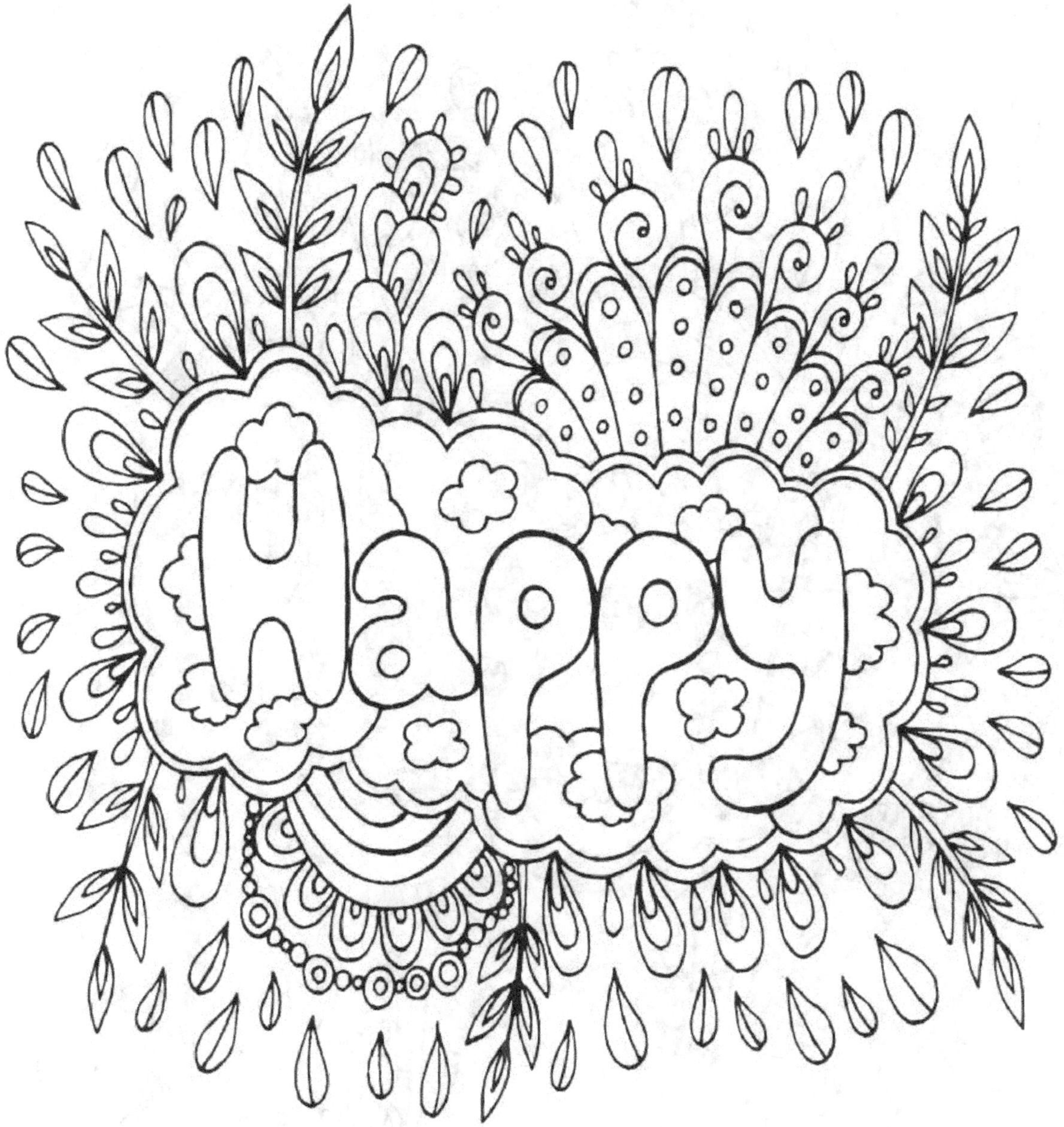
Happy

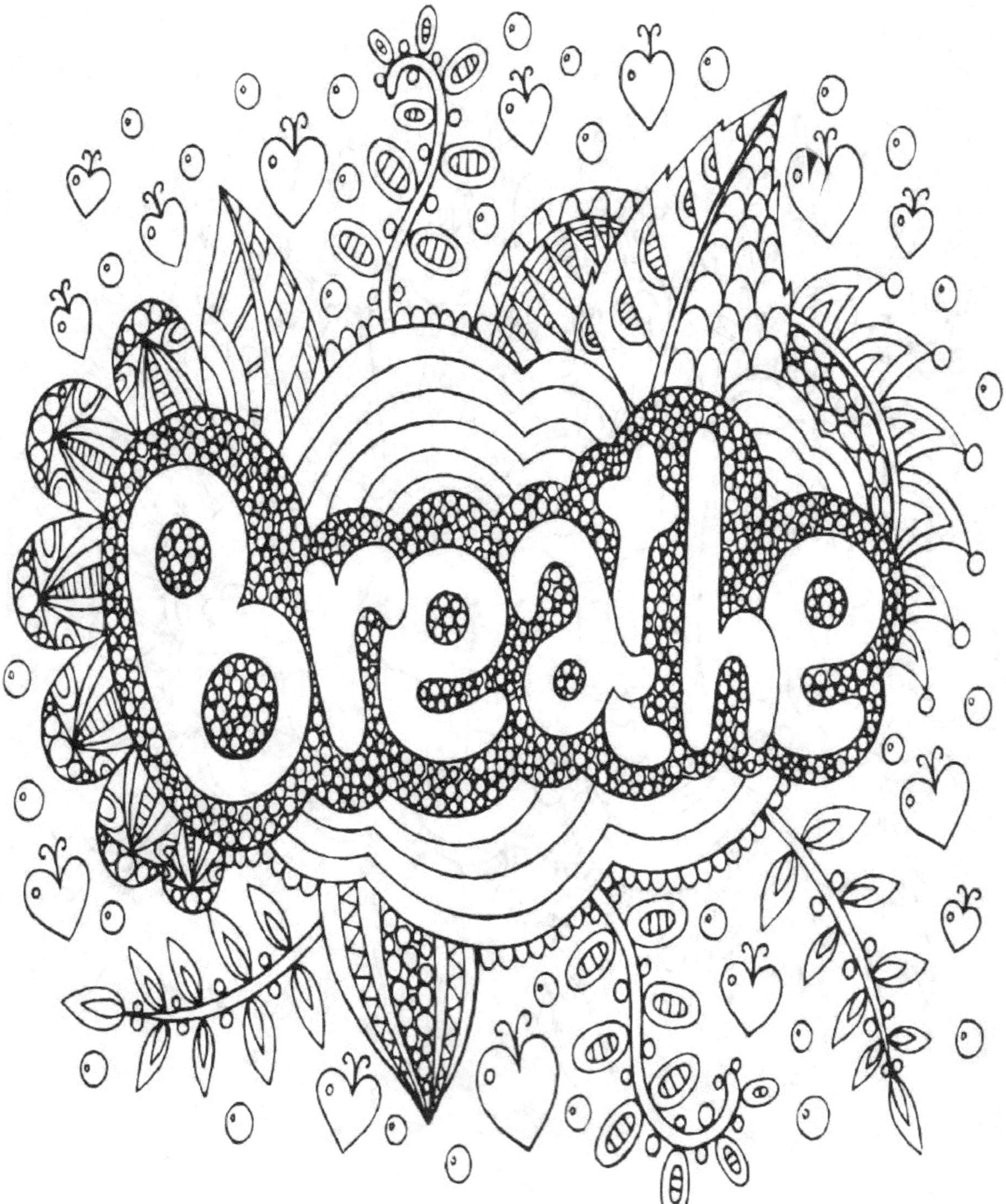
Breathe

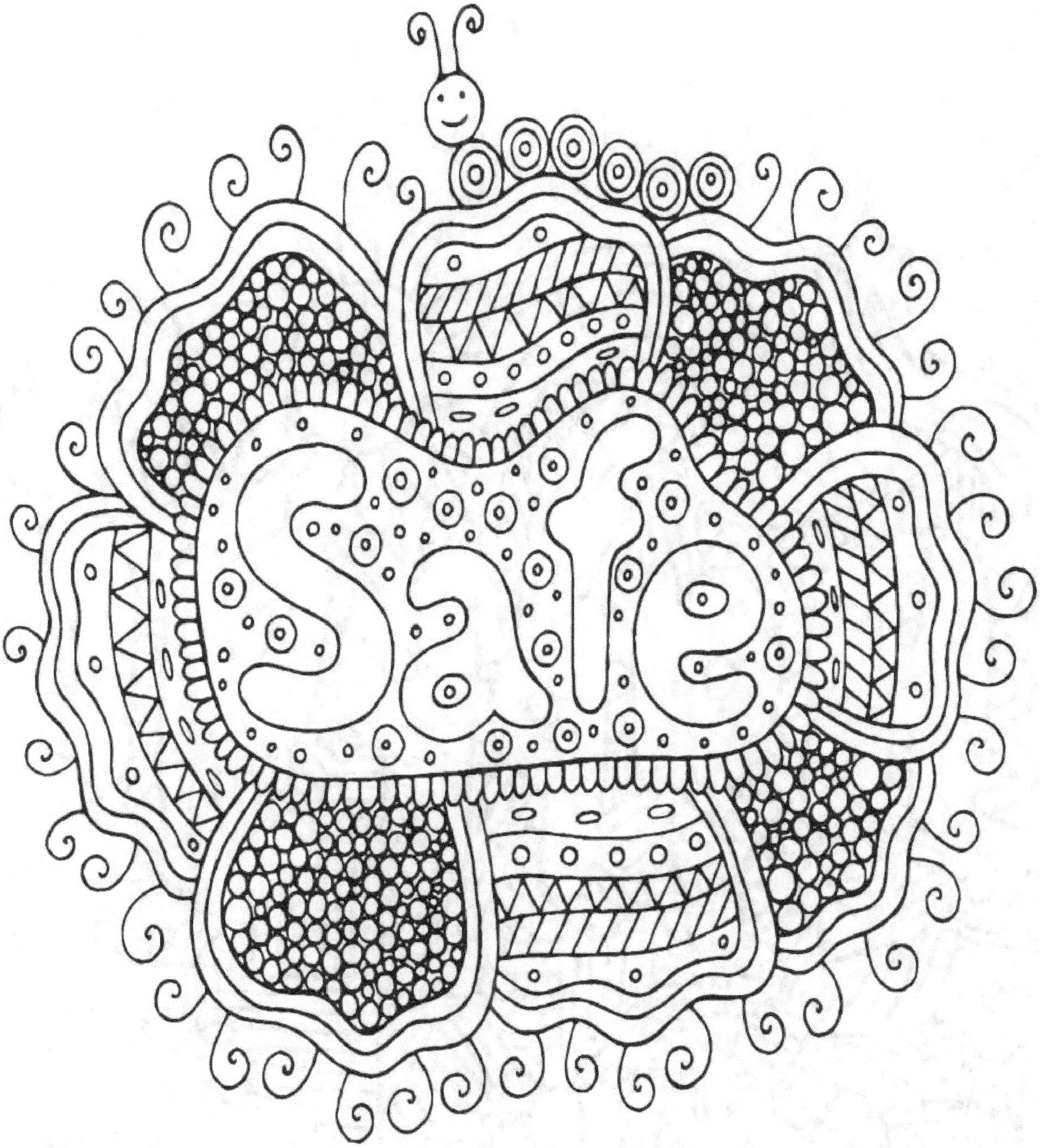
Safe

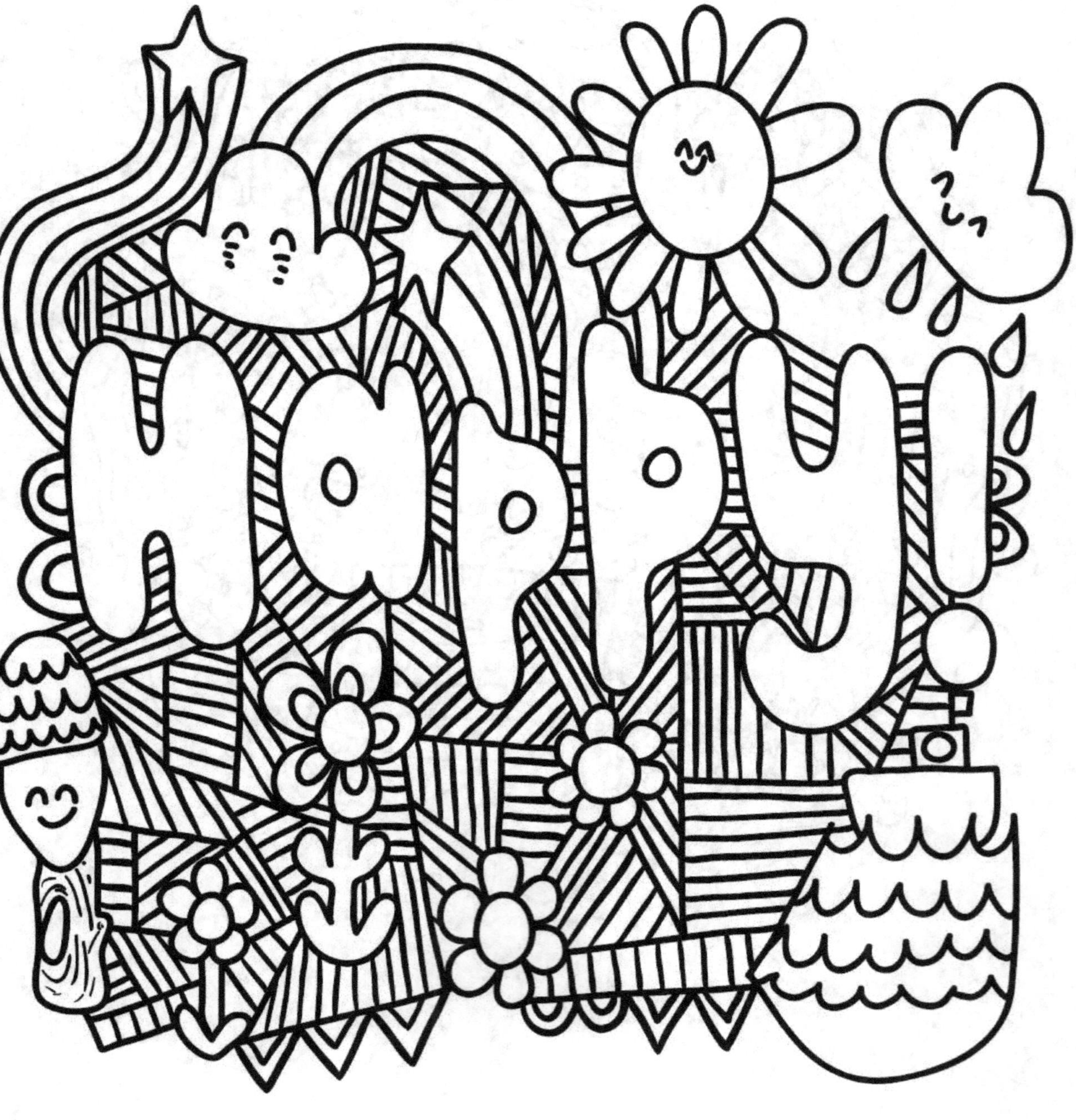
Happy!

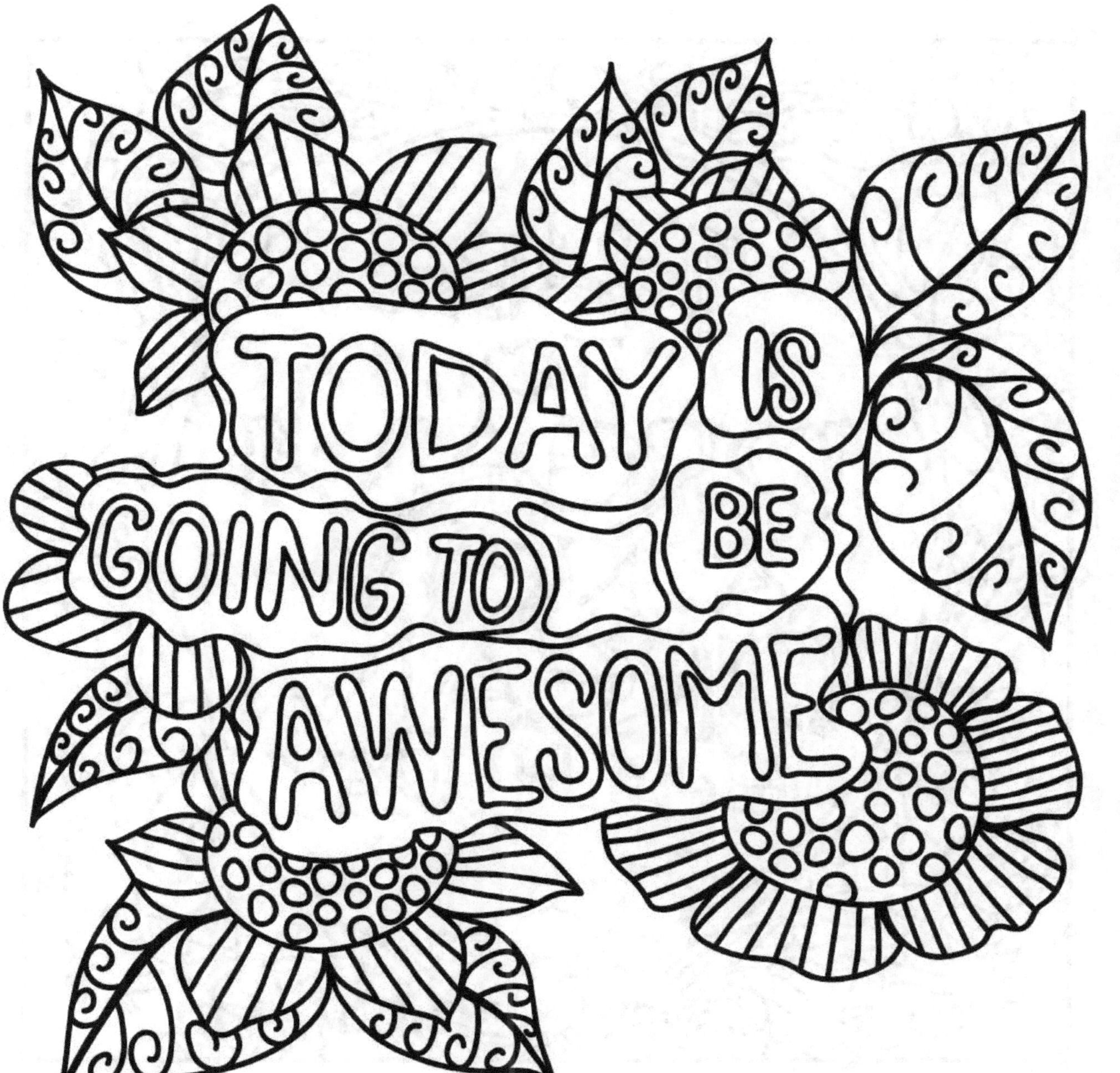
TODAY IS
GOING TO BE
AWESOME

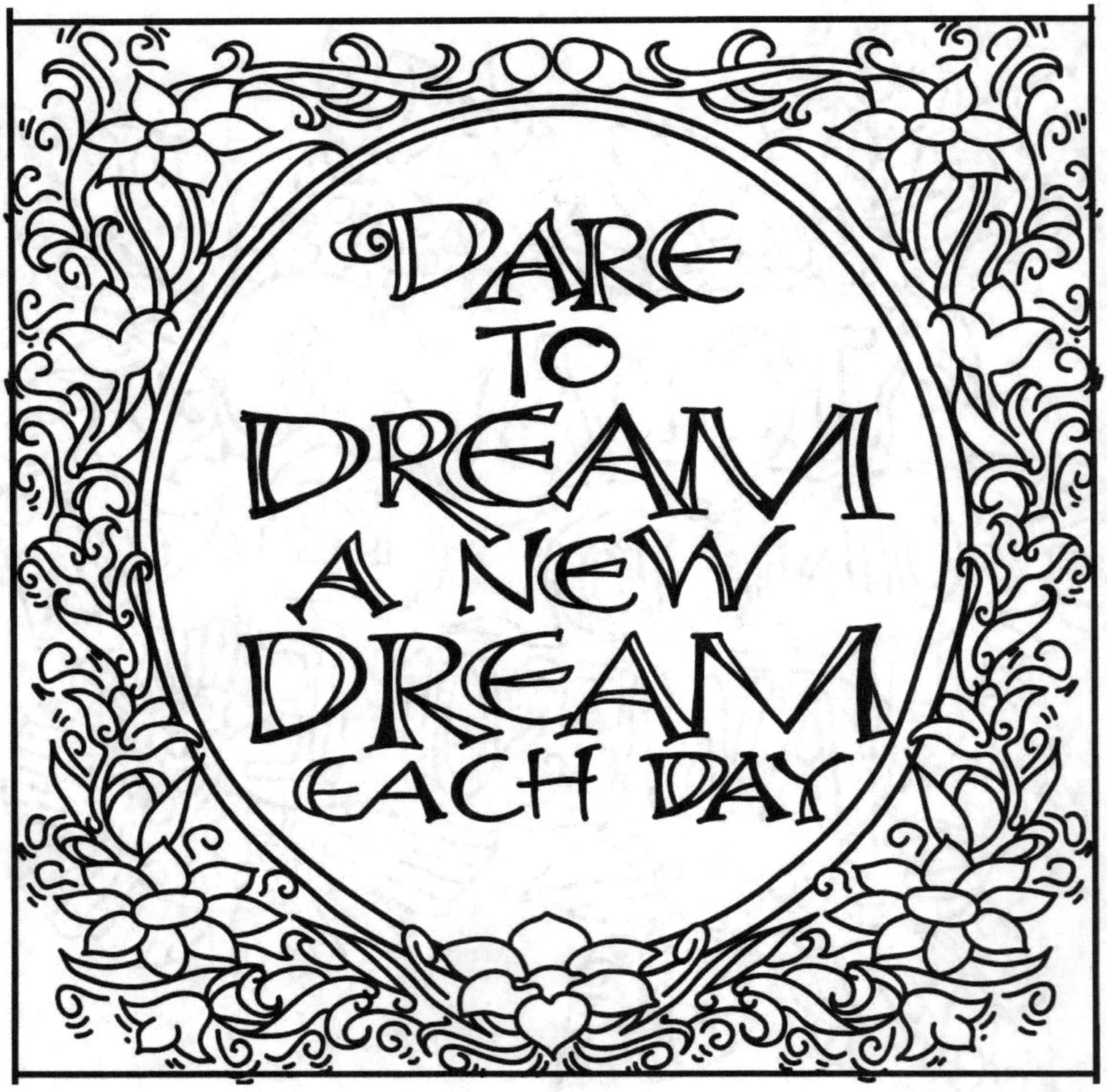
DARE
TO
DREAM
A NEW
DREAM
EACH DAY

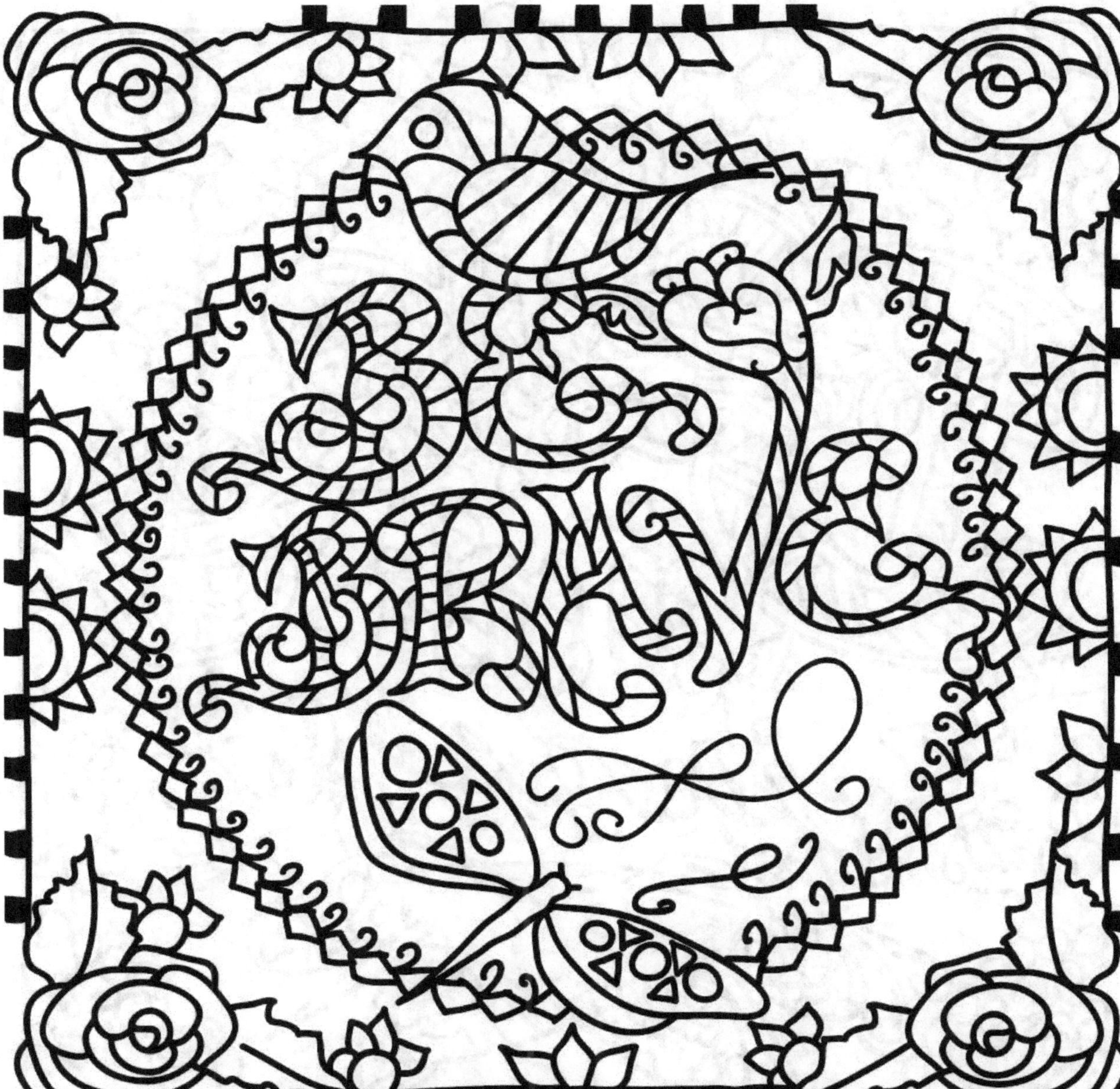

BE BRAVE

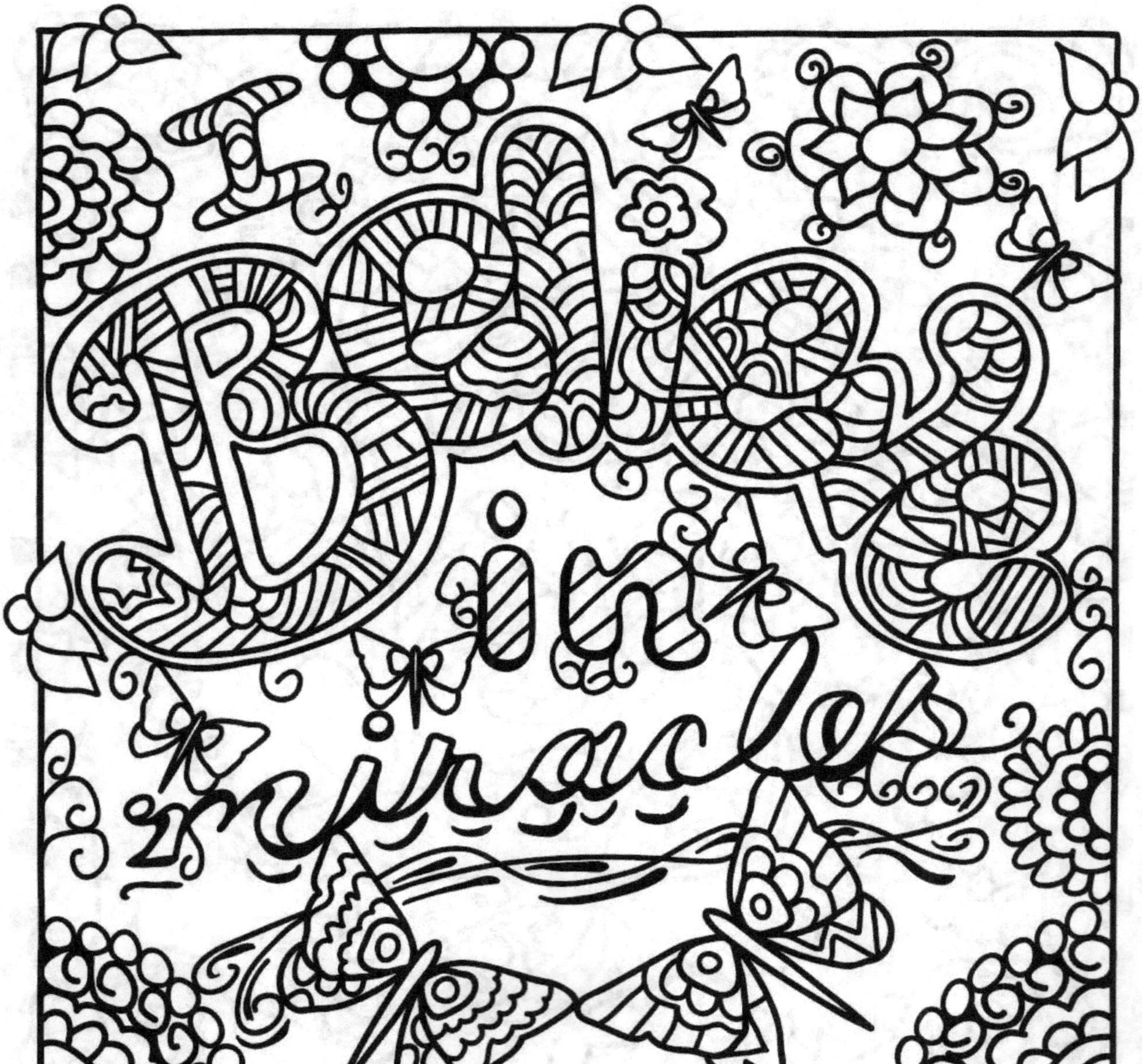
I Believe in miracles

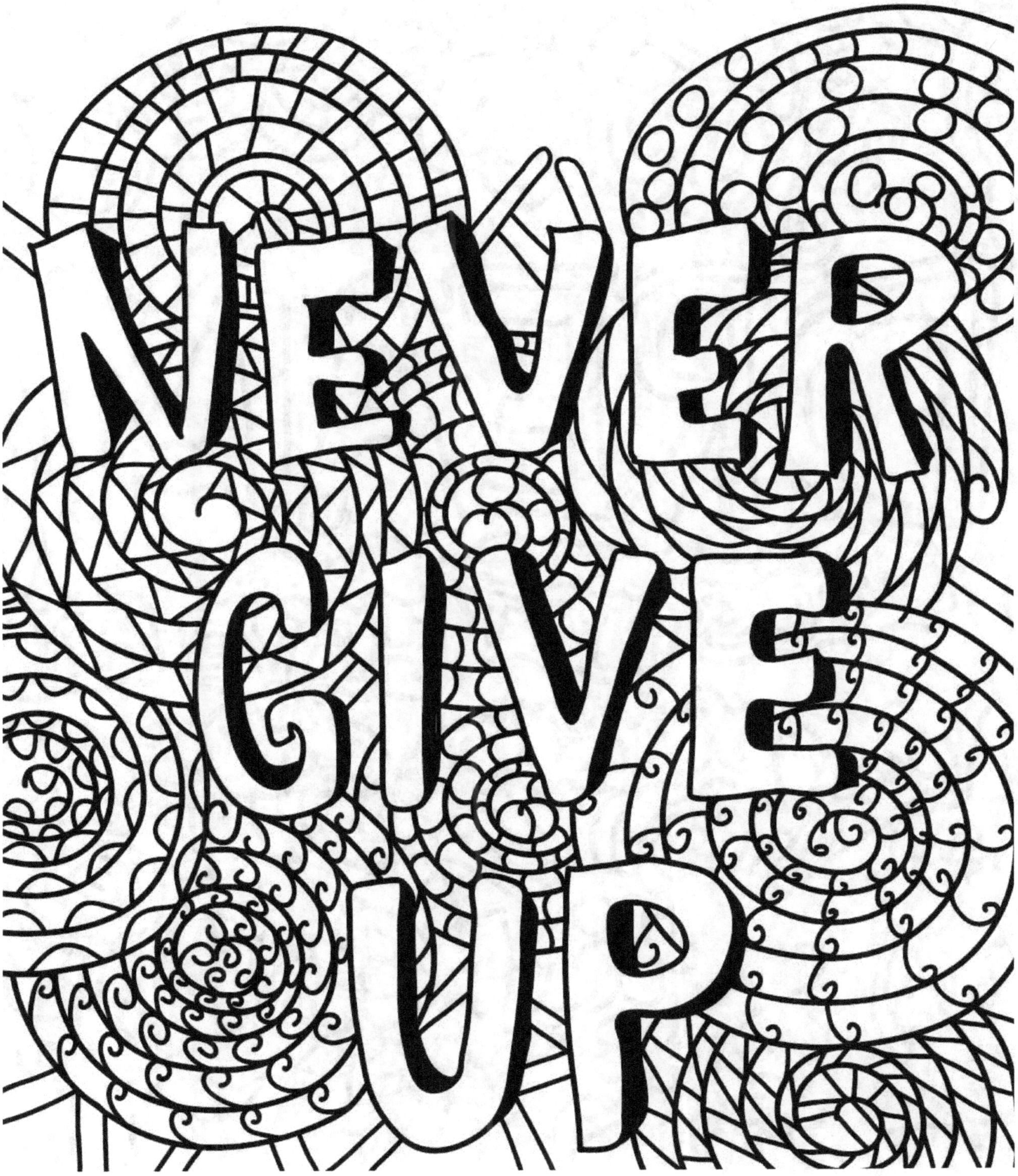
NEVER
GIVE
UP

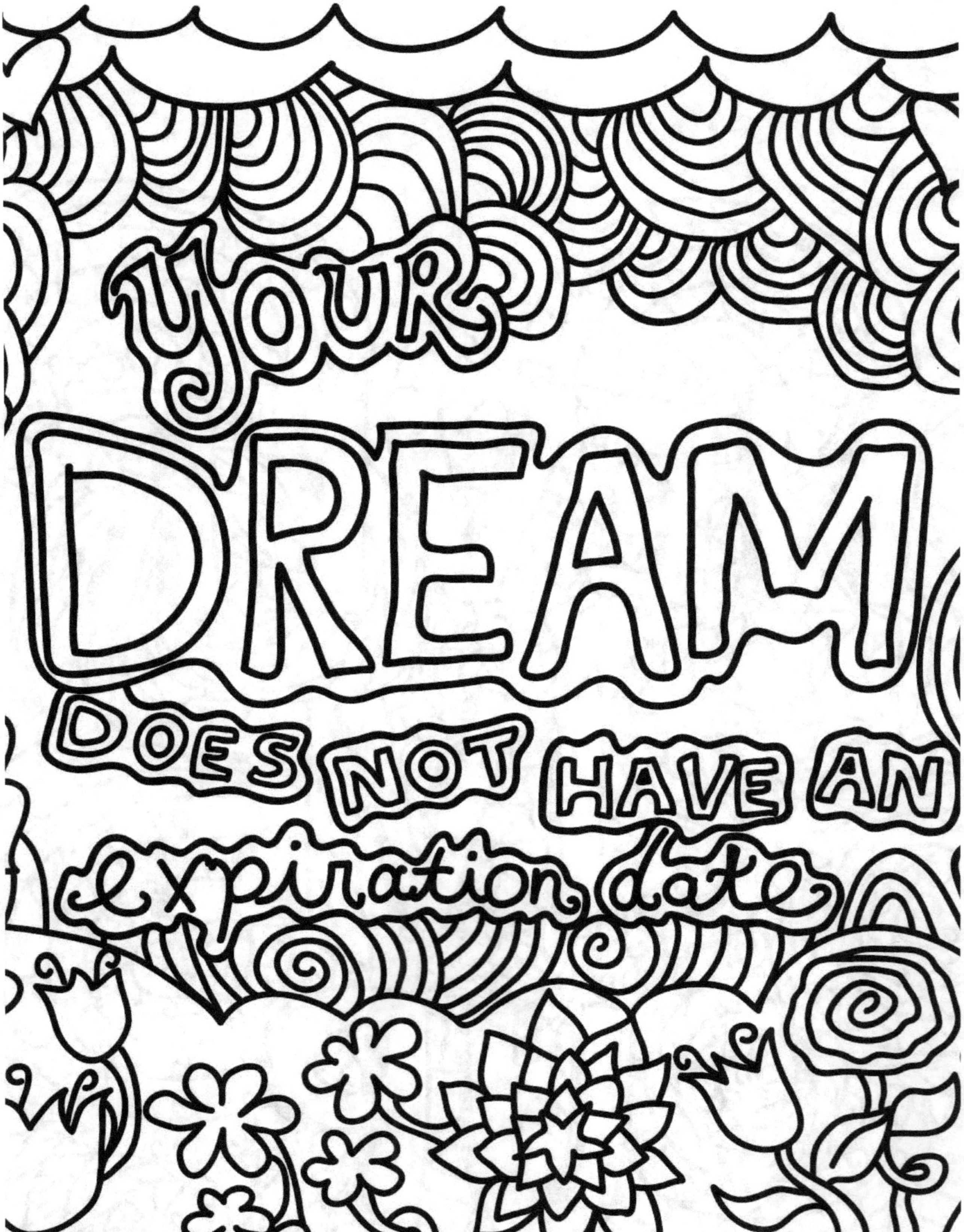
YOUR
DREAM
DOES NOT HAVE AN
expiration date

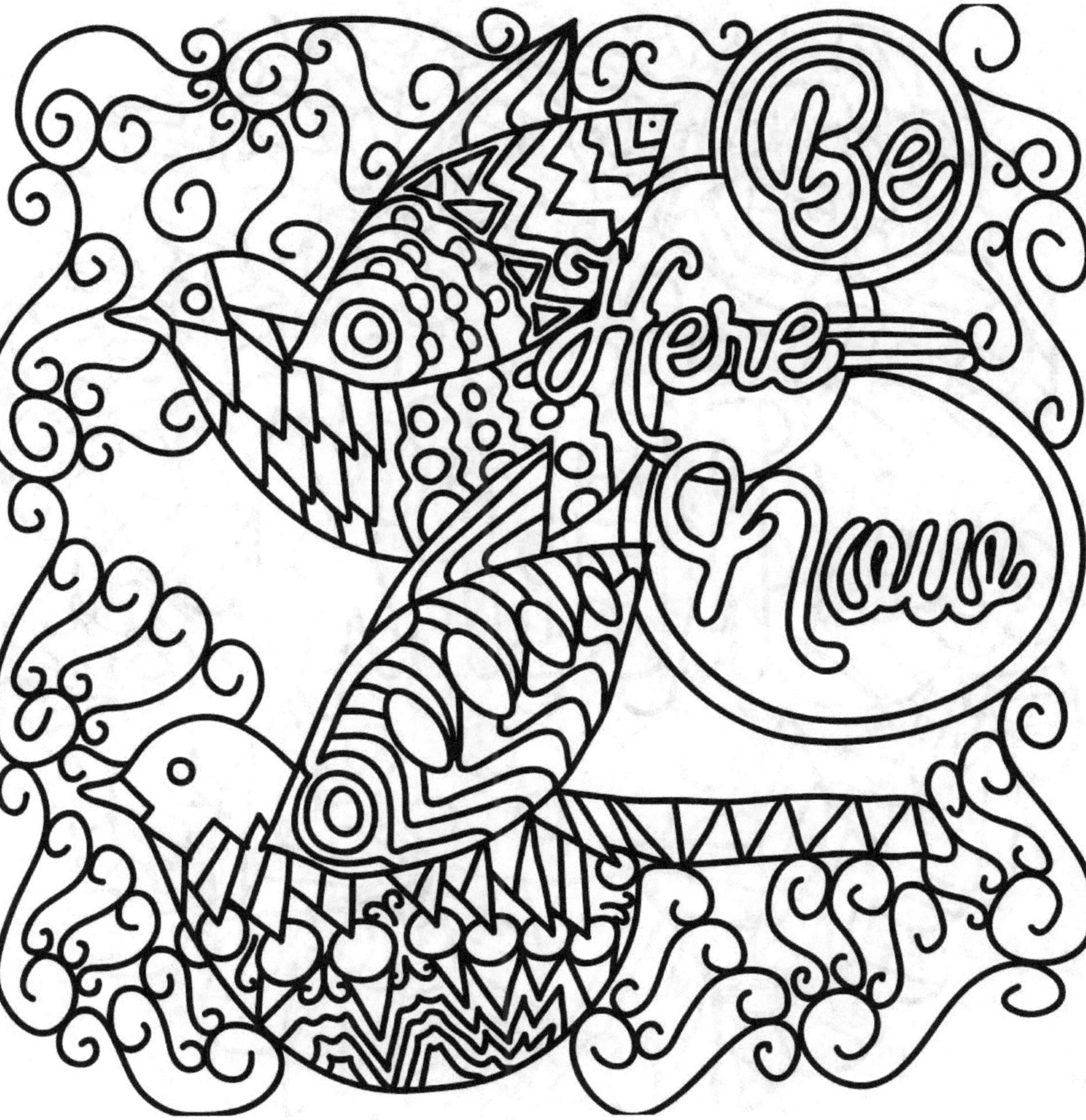
Be
Here
Now

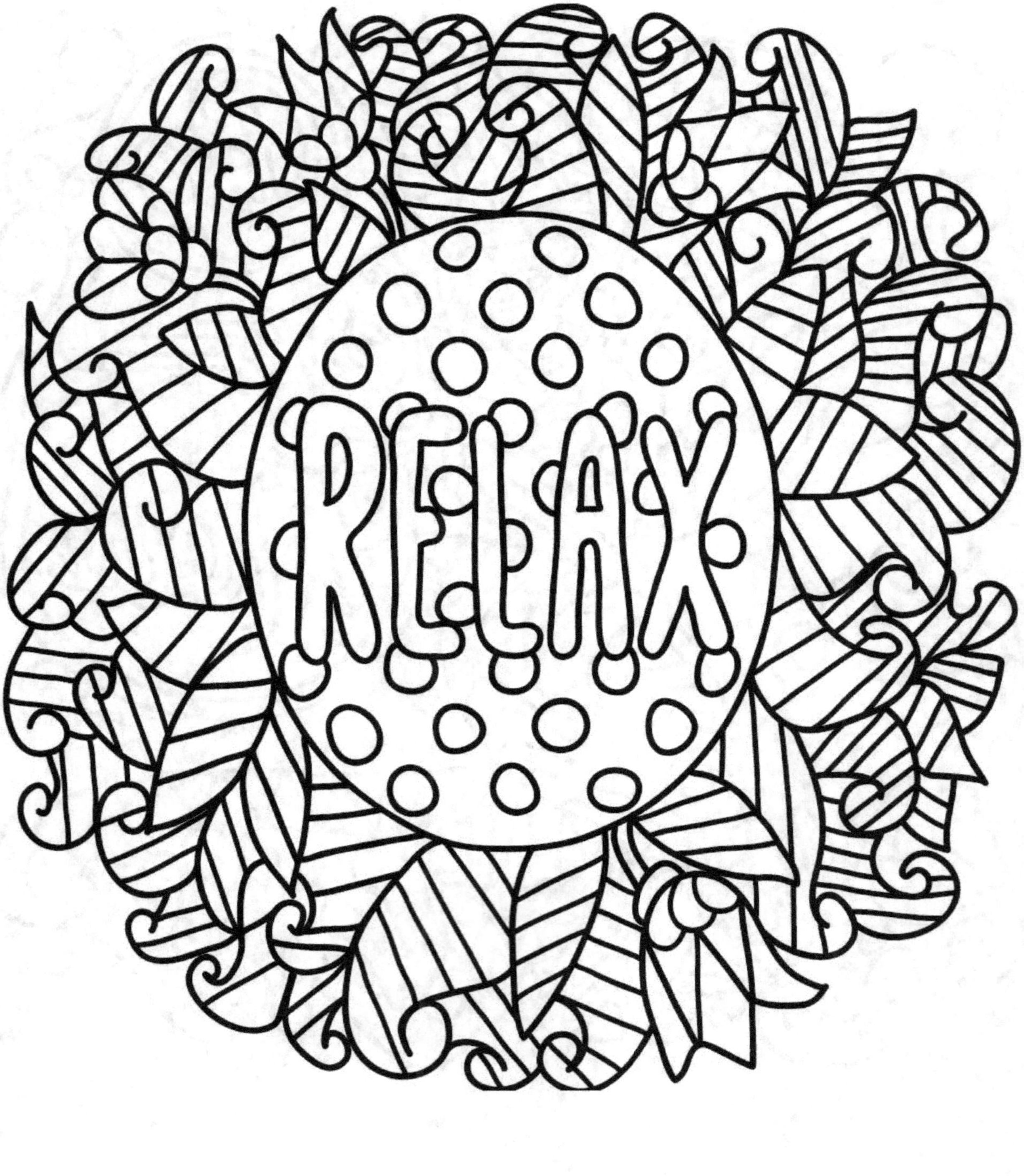
RELAX

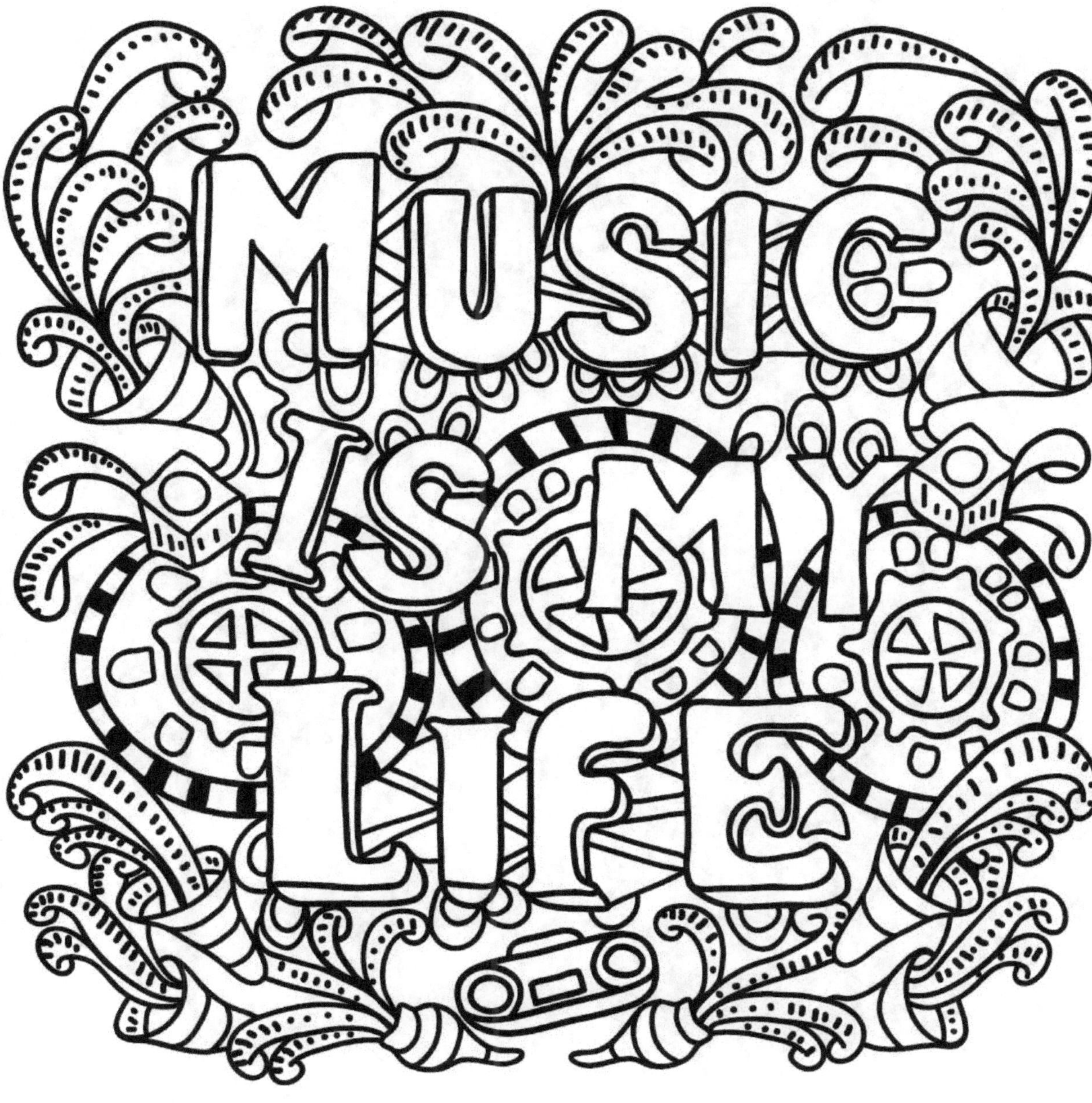
MUSIC IS MY LIFE

www.ingramcontent.com/pod-product-compliance
Lightning Source LLC
Chambersburg PA
CBHW080611220526
45466CB00010B/3315
* 9 7 9 8 5 2 9 8 4 6 8 1 0 *